MW01028178

FROM BLUE TO GRAY

Also by the author:

Debris of Battle:
The Wounded of Gettysburg

Rebels from West Point

Justice or Atrocity:
Gen. George E. Pickett and the Kinston, N.C. Hangings

From Blue to Gray

THE LIFE OF
CONFEDERATE GENERAL
CADMUS M. WILCOX

Gerard A. Patterson

STACKPOLE
BOOKS

Copyright © 2001 by Stackpole Books

Published by
STACKPOLE BOOKS
5067 Ritter Road
Mechanicsburg, PA 17055
www.stackpolebooks.com

All rights reserved, including the right to reproduce this book or portions thereof in any form or by any means, electronic or mechanical, including photocopying, recording, or by any information storage and retrieval system, without permission in writing from the publisher. All inquiries should be addressed to Stackpole Books, 5067 Ritter Road, Mechanicsburg, Pennsylvania 17055.

Printed in the United States of America
10 9 8 7 6 5 4 3 2 1

FIRST EDITION

Library of Congress Cataloging-in-Publication Data
Patterson, Gerard A.
    From blue to gray : the life of Confederate General Cadmus M. Wilcox / Gerard A. Patterson.—1st ed.
        p. cm.
    Includes bibliographical references (p.) and index.
    ISBN 0-8117-0682-6
    1. Wilcox, Cadmus M. (Cadmus Marcellus), 1824-1890. 2. Generals—Confederate States of America—Biography. 3 Confederate States of America. Army—Biography. 4. United States—History—Civil War, 1861-1865—Campaigns. I. Title.

E467.1.W65 P38 2001
973.7'13'092—dc21
[B]
                                                        00-059534

To Diane, comme toujours

Cadmus Marcellus Wilcox, late in the war. LIBRARY OF CONGRESS.

CONTENTS

ACKNOWLEDGMENTS

TRAILING CADMUS MARCELLUS WILCOX ON HIS LIFE'S JOURNEY FROM Tennessee to West Point, Mexico and Europe, his postings at U.S. Army forts in New York and the Southwest, his movements as a Confederate general and his postwar life in New Orleans, Baltimore, and Washington required the aid of numerous well-positioned and knowledgeable historians and librarians.

Each was able to provide some clue to Cadmus' whereabouts and activities at different points of his odyssey and gradually fill in the time gaps that initially seemed beyond accountability.

Some, naturally, were of more help than others in this biographical search and I would like therefore to thank particularly Jeffrey M. Flannery, manuscript reference librarian in the Manuscript Division, Library of Congress; Bailey Thomson of the journalism faculty, University of Alabama, Tuscaloosa; and Richard Breithaupt, Jr., president of the Aztec Club of 1847, Van Nuys, California.

Other individuals who provided or led me to key pieces of information were Chris Calkins, historian of the Petersburg National Battlefield, Petersburg, Virginia; Julia Rather, archivist, Tennessee State Library and Archives, Nashville; Jack D. Welsh, M.D., Oklahoma City, Oklahoma; Ray Brown, cultural resources specialist, Manassas National Battlefield Park, Manassas, Virginia; Dale Floyd, Springfield, Virginia; Alicia Maudlin, Special Collections and Archives Division, U.S. Military Academy, West Point, New York; Joseph Pozell, superintendent, Oak Hill Cemetery, Washington, D.C.; Dr. Richard J. Sommers, U.S. Army Military

History Institute, Carlisle, Pennsylvania; Kathryn Page, curator of maps and manuscripts, Louisiana State Museum, New Orleans; Ervin L. Jordan, Jr., curator of technical services, University of Virginia Library, Charlottesville, Virginia; Francis P. O'Neill, reference librarian, Maryland Historical Society, Baltimore; Sarah Keats, law library, Library of Congress; Robert K. Krick, chief historian, and Donald C. Pfanz, historian, Fredericksburg-Spotsylvania National Military Park, Fredericksburg, Virginia; Rebecca Roberts, public outreach services coordinator, University Libraries, University of Alabama, Tuscaloosa; and Frances S. Pollard, assistant director, Library Services, Virginia Historical Society, Richmond.

I am also indebted to the staffs of the Rare Book, Manuscript and Special Collections Library of Duke University, Durham, North Carolina, and the Southern Historical Collection of the University of North Carolina at Chapel Hill for their generous assistance.

The support and understanding shown me by William C. Davis, editor of Stackpole Books, whose own writings set a standard for all Civil War historians, and Leigh Ann Berry, associate editor, are also very much appreciated.

Gerard A. Patterson

INTRODUCTION

THE STORY OF A CONFEDERATE GENERAL WITH THE THEN-FASHIONABLE Romanesque name of Cadmus Marcellus Wilcox does not deal with some great Civil War leader. He was merely one of Robert E. Lee's nine infantry division commanders, and hardly the most distinguished. In the massive volume of information about that war, why then should the experiences of Wilcox demand any particular attention?

The answer lies in the personal perspective Wilcox provides on how the conflict tragically redirected the lives of some of its more reluctant participants. Wilcox was one of those Southern officers who had been to West Point, done well in the Mexican War, and had a promising career in the regular U.S. Army when, to his chagrin, he found himself being swept up in what was being regarded by his government as an armed rebellion. Leaving the "old army" to go with the Confederacy was, in Wilcox's case, a particularly difficult and wrenching step, because few officers were as universally popular as he or, for that matter, progressing as well. He had been abroad to study the European armies and had written a highly regarded work on military science. While still in his twenties, he had been assigned to the military academy to teach infantry tactics.

From a familiar life of commanding seasoned regulars at established posts, he had to adjust abruptly to a ragtag army of volunteers, composed of men whose social background made taking orders offensive and, to their eyes, discretionary. Somehow he had to quickly prepare them for the battlefield, an arena he was one of the few to have entered.

Wilcox did his work well, and the Alabama brigade he shaped became one of the Army of Northern Virginia's strongest units, contributing significantly to the victories at Gaines' Mill, Second Manassas, and Salem Church.

Through Wilcox, the professional soldier, we are able to see how in a newly forming army in which promotion came with dizzying rapidity, even the most dutiful officer could become greedy for further advancement and jealous of any junior passing him. His later difficulties in command of an entire division underscore the reality that only so much could be demanded of a man who had been but a captain before the war and was now clearly being pushed by necessity to the very limit of his capacity for command.

In Wilcox's forlorn foray into Mexico after the surrender at Appomattox to seek a place in Emperor Maximilian's French army, we can sense his desperation to somehow continue using the only skill he had acquired—the practice of arms. And in his personal ruin—a fall so pronounced that he, in middle age and as a former major general, had to accept work as a lowly messenger in the U.S. Senate fourteen years after the war—we can appreciate the plight of so many Southern leaders after the war.

But while Cadmus Wilcox shared much in common with the 305 other West Point graduates who sided with the Confederacy, he had his own private concerns and distractions to deal with throughout the conflict and afterward.[1] First and foremost was his constant worry about the welfare of his cherished sister-in-law and her two small children in far-off Texas after the sudden death of Cadmus's brother, Confederate congressman John A. Wilcox, in Richmond. The lifelong bachelor's solicitude for the family—to whom he was Uncle Cad—precluded his accepting lucrative positions abroad that would require lengthy separation.

The widow to whom he dedicated himself, even if unable to materially assist her, was the former Mary Emily Donelson, a gifted linguist and musician who provided a classic example of the family schisms the war created. She was born and raised in the White House, her father, Andrew J. Donelson, having served as Andrew Jackson's confidential secretary and advisor while her mother, Emily Donelson, fulfilled the social role of first lady for the president, a widower. Whereas Andrew Donelson staunchly opposed the secession movement and the break up of the Union, Mary Emily's brother and uncle became Rebel army officers.

Aside from the historic perspective Cadmus Wilcox provides, analysis reveals him as a very human, personable individual possessed of a wry, dry humor that is often charming; what seems to be a touch of hypochondria,

given the list of exotic ailments his letters catalogue; and a rather picturesque taste in military attire. (Although he was sometimes ornately uniformed, in the field he usually wore a battered straw hat and a short, round
jacket and rode a white pony, carrying a long hickory switch as a crop.)

While not performing whatever menial work was necessary for his
livelihood in the postwar years, Wilcox began compiling a detailed history
of the long-ago Mexican War in which, as a spirited lieutenant, he had had
a conspicuous part. The book, edited by his niece and published shortly
after his death, stood for decades as the definitive work. In it, Wilcox
almost always alluded to the event that subsequently divided his host of
army friends as "the late war," never the Civil War or anything as repug-
nant to him as the War of the Rebellion.

Throughout his years in Washington, Wilcox's social life was confined
mainly to old army friends, both Northern and Southern, especially the
Aztec Club, an association of army officers he cofounded in Mexico City
in 1847 and that was reactivated shortly after the Civil War. The meetings
of this exclusive society brought together an unlikely assemblage of figures
that might include, on any occasion, U. S. Grant and Joseph E. Johnston,
William T. Sherman and P. G. T. Beauregard.

A final poignant reunion came after Wilcox's death from an accidental
fall in 1890, when three former Confederate generals and three U.S. Army
generals served as pallbearers at his funeral. Virginian Harry Heth, one of
Wilcox's closest longtime friends, said of the man who had served all the
way from Manassas to Appomattox conscientiously, if not spectacularly,
that "he did his whole duty."[2]

The man depicted in this study was revealed mainly in the letters that
Wilcox, an active correspondent, wrote to relatives and army associates
over the years, often indiscreetly. These letters are now housed in libraries
and archives around the country, from the Library of Congress to the University of North Carolina. Wilcox's image is enhanced by the voluminous
papers of the remarkable family to which he became so much attached, the
Donelsons of Tennessee.

As one traces Cadmus Wilcox's experiences before, during, and after
the war, one comes to realize the personal destruction the conflict was able
to inflict on those never touched by a bullet, and how for some, the pun-
ishment for their involvement would never end.

CHAPTER ONE

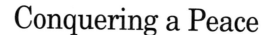

Conquering a Peace

As Cadmus Marcellus Wilcox, fresh from West Point, crossed the Rio Grande and made his way across the rugged, arid Mexican landscape to reach the 4th Infantry at Monterey, the twenty-two-year-old brevet second lieutenant had the concern of many young soldiers who had not yet been in combat—that the fighting might be over before he saw action.

Approaching his exotic destination, he could observe, as did another new arrival, how "the whitewashed walls and the flat-roofed houses, half hid by the dark green foliage of the palm, the orange and the cactus, with the picturesque towers and Moorish domes of the Cathedral, the chapel and convents, gave it more the appearance of an Oriental city than one of the New World."[1]

But Wilcox probably was more concerned with launching his first tour of active duty in impressive fashion than in noting the charms of his hardly warlike surroundings. "There seemed to be an impression that the war would terminate with the battle of Monterey and all who had seen field service, especially if they had been in battle, were regarded with high favor," Wilcox later recalled.

He thought it fortunate that the three messmates he joined when he reported for duty on October 23, 1846, in his new but already dusty regulation blue uniform with high, visored hat, "had been with the army at Corpus Christi, on the march to the Rio Grande and in the battles of Palo Alto, Resaca de la Palma and Monterey." They were Sidney Smith of Virginia, Jenks Berman of Vermont, and Ulysses S. Grant of Ohio.[2]

1

Cadmus Marcellus Wilcox, as a U.S. Army lieutenant in 1847. U.S. ARMY MILITARY
HISTORY INSTITUTE.

The eager young subaltern from Memphis was particularly drawn to
Grant, who had come out of the military academy two years before
Wilcox. The two remained friends for life. Wilcox's initial impressions of
Grant, who was called Sam, were that he was "quiet, plain and unobtru-
sive, of good common sense, with no pretension to genius or, as believed at
that time, to a high order of talent but much esteemed among his immediate associates for kindly disposition and many excellent qualities."[3]

Lt. Gen. Thomas J. Jackson, another of Wilcox's distinguished classmates. VIRGINIA STATE LIBRARY.

Lieutenant Wilcox, described at this time as "wiry, well-formed, dark complexioned" with "eyes as piercing as an eagle's," had come to Mexico with his academy class of 1846 almost en masse. No one in the group "had so many friends and was so universally esteemed" as Wilcox, with his "joyous, kindly nature." So exuberant a cadet had he been, in fact, that he ranked 186th in demerits among the 213 cadets at the academy the year he graduated.[4]

Wilcox had graduated fifty-fourth in his class. With him in Mexico were George E. Pickett of Virginia, who had finished fifty-ninth and last that year; Wilcox's brilliant friend George B. McClellan of Pennsylvania, who had graduated at the age of nineteen; the gawky, peculiar Virginian Thomas J. Jackson; Jesse Reno; and Darius Couch—all out to make their marks.

After graduation, Wilcox had had a brief furlough and traveled home in company with three classmates, one of whom was "Old Jack," as the cadets called their cold, undemonstrative classmate from Virginia. On their trip, Cadmus caught a glimpse of Jackson that he never revealed again. But it was one that provided the playful Wilcox with grounds for extortion if he chose.

The four had stopped over in Washington and took a room together just under the roof of Brown's Hotel. Wilcox was invited to spend the evening with Secretary of War William Marcy, a former governor of New York. How the invitation came about isn't clear, but Wilcox did not return from his engagement until 1 A.M. As he told the story to a friend:

> The door was locked, and the sounds of boisterous revelry were roaring within. For some time, he demanded entrance in vain, and when at last admitted found 'High Jinks' were enacting there. Poor Archie [Botts] in his fine new uniform, lay slumbering upon a bed, while Dominie [Wilson] and 'Old Jack,' with only one garment, were singing with stunning effect 'Benny Hahns' Oh,' and executing a barefooted back-step in time to the music. Each composed his own poetry, in tones which resounded through the house and over the Avenue, until the proprietor sent his compliments and a demand for quiet.
>
> This was Old Jack's first and last frolic, to which in years long after his fame had filled the world he dimly alluded when he said he was too fond of liquor to trust himself to drink it.[5]

It was memories such as this that made it difficult for the West Pointers to regard one another in the same way the men in the ranks looked upon their officers. They could see through every affectation and abruptly bring down even the most pompous by merely asking, "Do you remember the time when . . . ?" Perhaps it was their awareness of this vulnerability that led so many to keep their relations with men they had known since boyhood formal and reserved; the man who later became known as "Stonewall" Jackson was a prime example.

Now in Mexico, filled with nervous energy, Wilcox wasted little time in establishing himself with Gen. Winfield Scott's army. He was promoted to second lieutenant in the 7th Infantry on February 16, 1847, and was conspicuous at the battles of Vera Cruz, Cerro Gordo, and the advance on the City of Mexico.

In July, much to Wilcox's surprise and delight, he was invited by Maj. Gen. John A. Quitman, a political general from Mississippi, to join his staff as an aide-de-camp. It was a high honor for an ambitious junior officer so newly commissioned.

Under the eye of the division commander at Chapultepec, the lofty fortress guarding the approach to the capital, Wilcox and two other young officers daringly mounted the scaffold of the Belen gate to raise the Palmetto flag of a South Carolina unit and signal to the army the capture of that key entry point. Such heroics naturally began to attract heavy fire from the Mexicans, and General Quitman, mounted below, soon called up to Wilcox and the others, "That will do, get down."

"I jumped from the scaffold instantly," Wilcox wrote, "and as I reached the ground was considerably shocked, almost turned around by a musket ball striking a pistol at my left side, worn under the sash and sword belt. The ball flattened itself, fell to the ground and was picked up."[6] It was a perilously earned souvenir, but Wilcox's fiery dash at Chapultepec won him a brevet first lieutenancy for gallantry.

If he was pleased with his own performance thus far in his first exposure to warfare, he was also extremely proud of the skill displayed by the other West Pointers taking part, particularly members of his outstanding class. But one officer he encountered in Mexico whom he regarded with absolute awe was a forty-one-year-old captain of engineers, Robert E. Lee. Wilcox first made his acquaintance at the siege of Vera Cruz, later recalling: "I was much impressed with his fine appearance, either on horse or on foot. Then he was in full manly vigor, and the handsomest man in the army."

Whether it was making roads over difficult terrain to get the army in better position, situating batteries, or undertaking night reconnaissance, Lee's indefatigable enterprise was contributing to victory after victory, at Cerro Gordo, Contreras, Churubusco, and Chapultepec, and made the achievements of his fellow officers appear trivial. Lee's later prominence came as no surprise to Wilcox. "His success, great as it was, was only what had been anticipated," he observed after his close exposure to Lee in Mexico.[7]

To Wilcox, the Mexican War was a noble war and not one carried out mainly for expansionistic purposes, as many believed. "Responding to their country's call in the hour of danger, and commissioned by her to 'conquer a peace,'" he wrote of the men who took part, "they waged a contest

unique in American and unparalleled in historic annals. The only war in
which the United States forces ever invaded an enemy's country, occupied
its capital and held its territory by right of conquest, it is also the only one
ever undertaken by a nation to 'conquer a peace' and in which the material
advantages gained by the victors were counterbalanced by the political,
commercial and educational benefits accruing to the vanquished."

He maintained that the conflict with Mexico engendered "a national
prestige inspiring confidence at home and respect abroad. Its momentum
generated a force which flashing forth in 1861, removed the blot of slavery
from the national escutcheon and is not yet spent."[8] It was an odd connection to make, the Mexican War and the antislavery movement, but Wilcox
ascribed myriad benefits to the success there beyond territorial.

Once the fighting had stopped and Wilcox became part of an army of
occupation in the City of Mexico, the campaign was a very pleasant experience for the young officer. Although destined to be a lifelong bachelor, he
had an appreciative eye for the ladies. He was duly impressed with the
peerless climate of the Mexican capital, its tree-bordered promenades, the
theaters, and the bullfights, but also found the "dark eyed señoritas and
voluptuous señoras had many alluring attractions."[9]

At times, Wilcox was clearly appalled by the actions and behavior of
the triumphant army, and he was frustrated by the difficulty of managing
volunteer troops that have been given a measure of freedom. "Soldiers
commit many grave offenses, not cognizable by the rules and articles of
war, for which in their own country they would be tried by the civil courts
but if committed in a foreign land there is no tribunal before which they
can be brought."[10]

To provide themselves with a social gathering place, a group of idle
officers of the occupying army decided to form a society that would make
its "clubhouse" the mansion of Señor Boca Negra, the former Mexican
minister to the United States, on the Street of the Silversmiths. It began as
an affordable dining club for members and their guests, but soon it became
a place for the officers to drink liquor, smoke cigars, gamble at cards, and
otherwise consume their off-duty time while they waited to be withdrawn.
When, years later, Confederate general A. P. Hill was asked if he knew personally the Union general confronting him, Ambrose Burnside, he replied,
"Ought to, he owes me $8,000." Burnside was known to be as unlucky at
the card table as he was on the battlefield, and one might speculate that the
Aztec Club may have been where he incurred such an astronomical debt.[11]

The original 160 members of the Aztec Club included McClellan,
P. G. T. Beauregard, Joseph Hooker, Joseph E. Johnston, Philip Kearny,

John B. Magruder, George Sykes, and dozens of others who became prominent on one side or the other in a civil war only fourteen years distant. It was at the Aztec Club more than at the regulated West Point that the officers got to know one another well, sorting the brash from the timid, the quick-witted from the slow, the heavy drinkers from the abstinent. The convivial Wilcox was one of the cofounders. The men little imagined that the organization they established with mock formality on October 13, 1847, would still be active long after they were all gone and would be as valued by those who belonged as membership in the highest military order.

The easy life in slow, sunny Mexico came to a close in 1848, when the officers of the army of occupation began receiving new assignments back in the States. For Wilcox it meant garrison duty at Jefferson Barracks outside St. Louis, where he was happy to find he would again have the companionship of Sam Grant. He would also be serving with James Longstreet of South Carolina, whom they called "Pete" or "Dutch"; George Pickett; and several others he knew from either Mexico or West Point.

It was an uneventful period in which the proud, young officers could enjoy the laurels they had earned in Mexico. Time could be spent innocently in such activities as watching Grant's remarkable displays of horsemanship astride mounts others wouldn't dare approach or taking advantage of the opportunities for dissipation in lively St. Louis for those so disposed.

It was probably during this period that Wilcox found himself one day officiating at a christening with his friend and classmate D. N. Couch of New York. When Cadmus Marcellus Wilcox and Darius Narcissus Couch identified themselves for the minister performing the ceremony, he was taken aback. In fact, according to someone who heard of the incident from Cadmus, "it is said that when these sonorous designations reached the parson's ear he almost dropped the baby in round-eyed astonishment."[12]

A memorable occasion during this tour was the long-postponed marriage of Grant to Julia Dent, a cousin of Longstreet's and the daughter of a prominent slave-holding farmer in the area. Grant had become engaged during his and Longstreet's initial service at Jefferson Barracks before being sent to Mexico. Longstreet, who had introduced the couple to one another, was entitled to be a groomsman at the wedding, and Wilcox was asked by his former messmate to be another attendant. Until Appomattox, seventeen years later, it may have been the last time the three officers were together, for in 1849 Wilcox was ordered to Florida for service in the Seminole War, and Grant and Longstreet were dispatched in other directions. The three men shared an uneven relationship, however. While Grant was fond of both Wilcox and Longstreet and they of him, the two Southerners, for whatever reason, grew to dislike one another intensely. They came together often in the course of their lives, in various settings, but their mutual disdain never diminished.

On August 24, 1851, Wilcox, now with the 7th Infantry in Corpus Christi, Texas, was promoted to first lieutenant. In a small regular army in which even someone like Robert E. Lee could remain in grade as a lieutenant for eleven years and a captain for nine, Wilcox, just five years out of West Point, could look upon his career as proceeding well enough, though his current posting was a dull assignment.

Although Wilcox sometimes may have thought otherwise, he had not been forgotten in distant Texas by the army brass in Washington. On November 22, 1852, orders came for Wilcox to report to the U.S. Military Academy to serve as an assistant instructor of infantry tactics. The appointment coincided with that of now Brevet Colonel Lee as superintendent of the academy and brought Wilcox in close touch with the officer he so admired and who could presumably help his advancement, if indeed Lee had not already had a hand in Cadmus's receiving the choice faculty assignment at the rather young age of twenty-eight.[13]

During Lee's administration, the course of study was extended to five years, and several physical improvements were made to the academy and its surroundings, including a new wharf down by the majestic Hudson and construction of a spacious riding hall. Mainly, however, Lee concentrated on tightening cadet discipline at West Point, an effort in which Lieutenant Wilcox was an eager supporter.

After being named acting commandant—the number-two rank at the academy—Wilcox had charge of discipline and administration of the entire battalion of cadets for a while and demonstrated his authority in sometimes strange ways. He became part of the lore of the institution by his nocturnal practice of attaching rubber soles to his shoes to silently descend upon cadets smoking in their quarters, a common infraction. So notorious did Wilcox become with his stealth that a ditty was composed:

> "I hear the old rascal upon the stairs;
> In spite of his rubbers, I hear him there.
> He stole! He stole!
> He stole my pipe away!"[14]

Whether this could be counted as a form of amusement for the usually congenial Wilcox or he was playing the martinet with the plebes is unclear. As a regular army officer of six years' active duty who had already been in two wars and had a brevet for gallantry to his credit, some posturing may have been expected.

In May 1853, Wilcox wrote his family that all was going well for him at the academy, though one thing was bothering him, particularly because he was still such a young man: He was losing his hair.[15]

For most of the faculty members, the period at the academy between the Mexican and Civil Wars was one of the most pleasant times of their careers. A few years of active service had given them a chance to shed much of the rigid formality instilled during their own cadet days and they were able to relax and enjoy themselves when away from their classrooms. In fact, every time some new faculty member arrived whom they may have known from some prior service it was reason enough "to start the champagne corks popping."[16]

During the five years that Wilcox was at the academy, a procession of cadets came under his instruction, including a tall, rawboned youth from Kentucky named John Bell Hood, hardly a scholar; a not very good-looking boy from Virginia who went by the initials J. E. B. Stuart but whom his classmates facetiously had nicknamed "Beauty" Stuart; a bright Georgian by the name of Edward Porter Alexander who was appointed to the engineering faculty immediately upon his graduation; and a tough, dark-eyed, olive-skinned North Carolinian named William D. Pender, whom everyone called Dorsey.

To all these cadets, Wilcox, a seasoned veteran who had been to Mexico and on the frontier, was disciplinarian and mentor. An articulate, authoritative instructor who could reinforce his points by citing his personal observations in the field, he was at a level of knowledge and experience far beyond their own, and they jumped to their feet when he addressed them in class.

In 1856, Wilcox was superseded as commandant by Lt. Col. William J. Hardee, a Georgian who had recently finished a text entitled *Rifle and Light Infantry Tactics,* which would be broadly adopted. Perhaps Hardee's work inspired Wilcox to try to further his own career by making a literary contribution to military science, or maybe it was envy that his friend George B. McClellan was getting so much attention for his accounts of the Crimean War after being sent abroad by the secretary of war as an observer. But a year after Hardee's arrival at the academy, Wilcox took the bold step of requesting a yearlong leave of absence in order to go to Europe to study the methods of warfare being employed in the Old World.

Officially, Wilcox was granted leave on November 12, 1857, by the adjutant general's office for reasons of health, but he was given permission to spend the time in Europe, which would indicate that part of the therapy he needed was a change of routine and scene.[17]

Whatever the nature of his ailment, it was not debilitating enough to inhibit his voyaging to Dieppe and traveling on to Paris and other points. Wilcox dutifully reported his exact whereabouts to Washington every month. Though he no doubt enjoyed seeing the French capital, his professional interest was mainly in the army school at Vincennes, where he observed carefully the rifle instruction methods developed there. While abroad, he undertook a translation of a book on Austrian evolutions of the line and compiled a "Tabular Statement of the Composition of the French Army on a War Footing" drawn from the most recent official documents. (Wilcox, after some exposure at West Point, apparently had become quite proficient in French.) In his sea chest when he finally returned early in 1859 were a number of excellent French military works.[18]

On his return, Wilcox published a major work called *Rifles and Rifle Practice: An Elementary Treatise upon the Theory of Rifle Firing, Explaining the Causes of Inaccuracy of Fire and the Manner of Correcting It.* The study was the first of its kind and was considered so valuable that the War Department ordered 1,000 copies for distribution throughout the army. It also became a standard text at West Point.[19]

In his work, Wilcox demonstrated an extraordinary grasp of infantry tactics and was almost prophetic in describing how developments in the design of army rifles and ammunition, including the ringed minié ball, were going to revolutionize the conduct of warfare. He provided an accurate preview of what the fighting would be like when the American Civil War broke out two years later:

> The increased range and accuracy of the rifle, and the confidence with which it must inspire the soldier, will cause the fire of infantry to be far more destructive that formerly, and every enemy killed or wounded will no longer cost his weight in lead (or ten times his weight in iron, when killed by artillery).
>
> Fields of battle will be more extended than formerly. There will be more difficulty in estimating the variety and number of the adversary; more difficulty in properly placing troops on the field, and directing their movements. Keeping them together, holding them

well in hand so as mutually to protect and sustain each other will, in future, require the greatest care. As fields of battle will cover more ground than formerly, new tactical means to obviate the disadvantages resulting from this will be required; that continuity of lines required by tactics will no longer be necessary.

One can only wonder how much of what he had written came back to Wilcox a few years later at Gettysburg when he found himself on an exterior offensive line that extended more than seven miles.

Whereas infantry could once approach to within 300 yards of an enemy line without experiencing much loss, Wilcox pointed out, with the modern rifle fire is destructive at up to 1,200 yards and, when well directed, it becomes irresistible at 600 yards.

Wilcox's primary tactical advice was that "to shelter troops from the enemy's fire as long as possible without being too far distant, and to hold them well in hand, will probably be the best rule to observe."[20]

If making a contribution to military science was really the primary purpose of his unusually long leave, Wilcox had succeeded in making an impression on the army's high command, and a year after his return, he was promoted to captain and appeared to be well established in the officer corps.

Wilcox's prowess was particularly impressive in light of his background. His Connecticut Yankee father, Reuben Wilcox, a merchant, had relocated to Wayne County, North Carolina, where Cadmus was born on May 29, 1825, the second of four children. When he was two, the family moved to Tipton County, Tennessee. A few years later, Reuben died unexpectedly, leaving three small sons and a daughter for his wife, the former Sarah Garland, to raise on her own. Somehow she managed to send Cadmus to the University of Nashville, which he was attending when an appointment came for a cost-free education at the U.S. Military Academy, and he quickly altered his course.[21]

At about the same time, Cadmus's older brother, John A. Wilcox, who had been reading law with a local attorney, also left home, crossing the state line to start his own practice at Aberdeen, Mississippi, before he was even twenty-one years old. He soon became active politically in that state and was elected clerk of the state senate. When the Mexican War broke out, John went off with Col. Jefferson Davis as a lieutenant in the 1st

Mississippi Rifles, a regiment of volunteers who wore black slouch hats and red shirts outside their white duck pants. They were armed with Windsor rifles and carried eighteen-inch Bowie knives. John advanced to adjutant then lieutenant colonel of the unit that had gained fame at the battle of Buena Vista, and eventually he succeeded Davis in command of "Davis' Red Shirts." Forevermore, John Wilcox would be known as Colonel Wilcox, an appellation that surely must have galled his lower-ranking, West Point–trained younger brother.[22]

Moving in totally different directions, the Wilcox boys were doing very well for themselves, though in Cadmus's case the demands of a military career required that he exhibit a great deal of adaptability. When he returned to the army, it was to garrison duty at Fort Columbus in New York Harbor, a place where he spent a melancholy Christmas in 1859. Of the life of a professional soldier, he wrote at the time, "I have no home and the sad truth is brought vividly to my mind just at this particular season of the year."[23]

Though without either a mother or father now, Cadmus noted "I believe I have some good friends," and tried to content himself with that.[23]

After he had enjoyed the refinement of European capitals and the cosmopolitan ambience of New York City for some years, the army abruptly brought Wilcox back to the realities of the life he had chosen by sending him off to frontier duty against the Navajo in New Mexico in 1860.

Before leaving, however, Wilcox had a very pleasant social responsibility to fulfill. He had been invited by his close friend, George B. McClellan, to serve as senior groomsman at his wedding in May 1860 in New York. McClellan, out of the army now and a successful railroad executive, was marrying the popular Ellen Mary Marcy, adored by many young officers, particularly Ambrose Powell Hill of Virginia, who was also to be a groomsman. Miss Nelly was the daughter of Maj. Randolph B. Marcy, a career officer. Wilcox later wrote, "I know his [McClellan's] wife and her mother and father well, they were my most intimate friends in the old army."[24]

At Fort Fillmore, near La Mesilla, in the vast, open stretches of the Southwest, Wilcox busied himself (to the amusement and guffaws of the enlisted men, no doubt) in mastering a revolutionary new method of field communication. This was the wigwag flag signaling system, introduced by Maj. Albert J. Myer, and Wilcox was among the first officers in the army to learn it.[25] Wilcox was not one to idle away his time. However dull his posting, he always found ways to improve himself professionally and advance. He must advance.

Gen. and Mrs. George B. McClellan, at whose New York wedding Wilcox was senior groomsman. VIRGINIA STATE LIBRARY.

At a time when Wilcox's career could not have been progressing more enviably, and when he must have felt assured of his future in the army, alarming reports began arriving belatedly at his and other distant frontier posts of the worsening political situation back in the States that was threatening to break up the Federal Union. Having been so recently stationed in New York City, he had a sense of the mood in Yankeedom toward the South and the concern there over the direction affairs were moving on questions ranging from slavery to secession.

Now a momentous decision was rapidly approaching for Wilcox and the 165 other academy graduates from the Southern states then on duty with the Regular army. For the few who were politically active and felt

strongly the grievances of their section, their course was clear. Most, however, were far removed from the controversies and were doing little to pro-
mote or discourage disunion beyond engaging in quarrels at the officers'
mess. With time, ties to home states had become more and more tenuous.
It is doubtful that Wilcox had returned to Tennessee more than a few times
in the twenty years he had been in the military; now he regarded the army
as his home.

Richard S. Ewell, a captain of dragoons at the time, explained the pre-
vailing attitude among the Regular army officers this way:

> Every one here is on the tenter hooks of impatience to know
> what the Southern States will do. . . . Officers generally are very
> much averse to any thing like civil war, though some of the younger
> ones are a little warlike. The truth is in the army there are no sec-
> tional feelings and many from extreme ends of the Union are the
> most intimate friends.[26]

The career consequences of taking sides in the looming conflict, which
they all were under enormous pressure to do, were almost imponderable.
To leave the army meant giving up the investment of years of service and
hard-earned advancement, pensions, and security. As Ewell, sweating out
developments at a post in the Southwest, put it to a member of his family,
"I look to the business with particular dread because every cent I have in
the world may be lost in the distress and trouble of civil war."[27]

A newly forming Confederate army might offer the immediate
promise of lofty rank, but what sort of an amateurish military force would
they be directing? Taking up arms against the government of the United
States was a chilling prospect, and what would become of them as commissioned officers if the struggle for Southern independence should fail?

Wilcox, though opposed to the institution of slavery, nonetheless supported the secession movement, but it is not clear if that alone dictated his
decision. He could have gotten little guidance from his fellow officers,
because he had as many Northern friends who would stand firmly with the
Federal government as he had chums from Dixie who were merely waiting
for the appropriate moment to "go South." Though his classmate John
Gibbon of North Carolina sensed such an obligation to the Union that he
remained in the U.S. Army while three brothers enlisted in Confederate
units, the sentiments of Wilcox's family and the thought of having to stand
against his own kin if Tennessee left the Union were probably the strongest
factors in his decision, as they were for so many others whose most fervent
wish was that the issues could be resolved before they had to make a choice.

Wilcox's one hope was that the Federal government would simply permit the seceding states to leave the Union and not use force to bring them back. The man whose opinion he apparently valued most was his friend George B. McClellan, and when he contacted him on the subject, McClellan told him candidly to "stick to the Union to the last for it is both right and politic."[28]

Wilcox's moment of decision came on June 8, 1861, the day after mail reached the remote Fort Fillmore from San Antonio with the news that North Carolina, the state where Cadmus was born, and Tennessee, where he was raised, had seceded. At the same time, he also received an order to report to Lt. Gen. Winfield Scott in Washington. Such a directive from the commanding general summoning him to the nation's capital could only mean that Wilcox was to be placed in some very important position in the army. His career was suddenly at a crossroads, and Wilcox faced the most significant decision of his life. Washington was an ambitious officer's most prestigious posting. How could he pass up such a reassignment? In the morning, after what must have been a night of anguish, Cadmus sat down and wrote the briefest of notes to the adjutant general in Washington—one sentence that would change the course of his life forever: "Sir, I have the honor herewith to tender the resignation of my commission in the Army of the United States."[29]

For those leaving the service, such terse communications were more than a mere formality. By submitting them, the withdrawing officers believed they were relieving themselves of all obligations to the government and absolving themselves of the oaths of allegiance they had taken, in the event that any action was contemplated against them. But only the outcome of the fast-approaching war could really determine the validity of the Southern officers' argument. If their side won, it would not be an issue, but if they should be on the losing side, they would have to wait and see how the government intended to treat them. In an emotional sense, it is difficult to imagine that any of these men felt that the attachment to the "old army," its institutions, and the flag they had watched raised each day at one post or another could be so easily severed with the stroke of a pen.

Before leaving Fort Fillmore, Wilcox carefully packed up his set of French military works and shipped the books to his brother John. Much had changed in the elder Wilcox's life, too, since he had returned to Aberdeen, Mississippi, from Mexico as Colonel Wilcox. Now a familiar figure in the state, John decided to run for office and was elected to a seat in Congress in 1851 as a Union Whig, defeating the incumbent, Winfield Scott Featherston. His tenure in the House of Representatives, however, was brief. Failing to win reelection, Wilcox concluded that it was time for another change of scene, and in late 1853 he relocated once again, this time to Texas. He opened a law office in San Antonio, a lively town with a mixed English, Spanish, and Indian population still under 5,000 but growing rapidly with the influx of German and other immigrants. Reigniting his political career there, John was a presidential elector for the Know-Nothing party in 1856, but in 1858 he attended the state Democratic convention, returning to the fold. After the election of Lincoln in 1860, Wilcox, who had been lukewarm on disunion early on, became a delegate to the Texas secession convention and served on the committee that drew up the ordinance of secession. Now he was campaigning for a seat in the first Confederate Congress.[30]

Described as "a handsome, jovial fellow, popular with men, women and children," he was said to have owed what political success he enjoyed to "his wit, humor . . . and to his personal magnetism." A ready orator, he delighted listeners with his cleverly phrased anecdotes. But not everyone appreciated his style; one politico regarded John as "a man of low taste" disposed to mock "pious things."[31]

The anguish that the Wilcox family felt over the nation's dissolution stemmed from John A. Wilcox's marriage into Tennessee's renowned Donelson family. His wife was Mary Emily Donelson, whom he had married in Washington during his single term in Congress a decade earlier. She was the daughter of Andrew J. Donelson, a member of the West Point class of 1820 who had gained prominence not in the military but afterward in politics. A nephew of President Andrew Jackson, Donelson had long served as Jackson's private secretary and trusted advisor.

When the widowed Jackson moved into the White House, he invited the wife of Andrew Donelson to serve as first lady, and though she was but twenty-one at the time, Emily Donelson's high intelligence and training enabled her to quickly put things in order and cope admirably with her responsibilities, which included the management of a staff of eighteen servants. It was under these circumstances that Mary Emily Donelson was born in the White House on August 31, 1829, in a corner room facing Pennsylvania Avenue. Her christening took place in the East Room, with President Jackson and Martin Van Buren as godfathers. In addition to members of Congress and the cabinet and the diplomatic corps, the guests included a young lieutenant of engineers, Robert E. Lee, and his new bride, Mary Custis Lee, whose family estate was just across the Potomac at

Arlington.[32] Mary Emily grew up playing hide-and-seek in the rooms of various hues in the executive mansion and became the president's little darling. He called her "the Sunshine of the White House," and she accompanied him on numerous vacation trips. In a gesture of fondness, the president gave Mary Emily, when she was three, an eight-year-old mulatto slave named Emeline to serve as her personal attendant.[33]

Surrounded from birth by dignitaries, Mary Emily began at an early age to maintain a small, gold-adorned album, in which President Jackson made one of the first entries and to which Mr. Van Buren also contributed. Mary never forgot those years when her mother (who died tragically at the age of twenty-eight) was mistress of the president's house, particularly the holiday seasons. She later wrote:

> Through the mists of years I recalled a Merry Christmas in my childhood's home long ago, and sweeter than music across still waters come memories of the blessed influences voicing in that historic mansion on that memorable occasion the glad tidings from Bethlehem: peace on earth, good will towards men.[34]

Mary's older brother, Andrew J. Donelson, Jr., attended the military academy during the same time that Cadmus Wilcox was a cadet there, and they no doubt were well acquainted. Graduating second in the class of 1848, Andrew was appointed to the corps of engineers, the most coveted assignment. He went on to serve as an assistant instructor of practical military engineering at the academy from 1852 to 1858, during the period Wilcox was on the faculty there. Sadly, the young man's brilliant military career ended with his death at Memphis on October 20, 1859 at the age of thirty-three.[35]

Mary Emily's association with Washington did not terminate with Jackson's presidency. After living for a time at Jackson's Hermitage and attending Nashville Female Academy, she accompanied her father abroad in 1846 when he was appointed minister to the kingdom of Prussia by President James Polk. Only about seventeen years old when she left, Mary Emily used the opportunity for her cultural development to the fullest. During her nearly five years in Europe, she studied French, German, Spanish, and Italian, as well as music under the pianist and composer Kullak. Her travels and stays at various capitals on the Continent were filled with high adventure and memorable meetings with the famous. In Paris, she was in the audience at the Theatre Français when the renowned Rachel gave her first recitation of "La Marseillaise." In Berlin, she witnessed a revolution in the streets. During a winter in Italy, her father's position enabled her to meet Garibaldi, Pope Pius IX, and the king of Sardinia. In Madrid, she was presented to Queen Isabella.[36]

The young lady's excitement about all she was experiencing bubbled over in her newsy letters to her other brother, John, at home in Memphis. From Frankfurt, she wrote: "We have made already a great many agreeable acquaintances & lead a much gayer life than we did in Berlin. The Rothschilds . . . and other Frankfurt grandies have been very polite to me & have invited us several times to tea."[37]

But it was the museums and libraries of the Old World where she was most enraptured, and from Baden she wrote to John after examining some papers of Luther, "I always feel in a library as if standing amid the spirits of a thousand great and talented men whose legacies are the books around me."[38]

When the Donelsons finally returned to America, it was to Washington, where in 1851 Mr. Donelson became editor of the "Union Signal," the organ of the Democratic party. It was not until after 1856, when Donelson was the unsuccessful vice-presidential candidate on the Fillmore ticket, a defeat that effectively ended his political career, that he went back to Tennessee, but without Mary Emily. Shortly after her return to Washington, she had met Congressman John A. Wilcox at the Assembly Ball, and after the briefest of courtships, they were wed at the Donelson residence. The list of guests at the nuptials was dazzling and included Daniel Webster, General Winfield Scott, Stephen A. Douglas, and James Buchanan.[39]

Decades later, an undated newspaper article was found in Mary Emily's scrapbook indicating that the marriage to John A. Wilcox was more her father's choice than her own, and that her true love was a brother of President Polk's with whom she was eloping when Andrew Donelson intervened. Without mentioning Mary Emily by name, the Washington letter described her as "a beautiful young lady, as pleasing in manners as she was attractive in person. She was conspicuous in society. Men prominent at that time were her escorts."

According to the newspaper piece, Mr. Polk

fell in love with her, sought her hand in marriage and was accepted. He was a handsome man and possessed of more intelligence than his brother, who served as chief executive. The young lady's father opposed the proposed match and urged his daughter to accept the attentions of a Texas congressman. The congressman pressed his suit and, though the young lady loved Polk, in respect to her father's wishes she consented to marry him.

But Polk would not give up easily.

One afternoon while she remained alone at home, Polk called for her in a carriage, and she agreed to go with him to the residence of a minister, who lived on Capitol Hill. As the carriage containing the two was being driven along Pennsylvania Avenue, her father stood in front of the old National Hotel. He saw the two young people and, rushing to the street, stopped the horses. He ordered his daughter to alight, addressed a few emphatic words to her companion, and taking her arm hurried her into his home. In a short time her marriage to the Texas congressman was announced.

The husband, the item noted, "was an unattractive man, and was possessed of a most violent temper. The marriage was not a happy one." Who could possibly have been the source of such a detailed, intimate story if not Mr. Polk, or more likely, Mary Emily herself?

Only two years after her marriage, this worldly, sophisticated, and cultured young woman was taken by her husband to San Antonio, at the time the antithesis of refinement, where her two children were born, first Andrew on November 20, 1854, and then Mary Rachel, often called Molly, on November 14, 1857. Though living in distant Texas, Mary Emily's attachment to the nation's capital, the center of her own life for so many years, remained strong.

The schism in the Donelson family as civil war erupted stemmed from the fact that sixty-two-year-old Andrew Donelson had been so intimately associated with the president who had made the preservation of the Federal Union his sacred trust. There was no way that Donelson could bring himself to support the secession movement in Tennessee, "Old Hickory's" very own state, and he became deeply despondent over the course of events. To complicate matters further, Mary Emily's uncle, Daniel Smith Donelson, took an entirely different stand. Early on, Daniel, a planter who was still another graduate of West Point (class of 1825), accepted a commission as a brigadier general in the forming Confederate army. Young John Donelson, who had been up North to Yale, was a second lieutenant in a company called the Hickory Rifles.

Once an invasion by the Federal troops was threatened, old Andrew Donelson—though as vehemently opposed as ever to secession—dramatically altered his attitude toward the Federal government's policy and appeared to be now fully in favor of armed resistance. He even joined the home guard to "protect the families who may be left without defence."[41]

Donelson revealed his deep apprehension about the approaching conflict in a long letter to Mary Emily on May 26, 1861, from his Memphis
residence:

> I have heard nothing from you and Rachel [his other daughter]
> for a long time and am quite uneasy when I think of the troubles
> which surround you. Everything here is preparation for war. Men,
> women & children are all partaking of the excitement, and from
> what we hear the friends of Lincoln are determined to carry their
> policy at the point of the bayonet. By today's telegraph we learn that
> the Federal troops have commenced the invasion of Virginia and we
> may expect a similar movement toward Memphis from Cairo . . .
>
> These are indeed alarming times, such as we have never known
> before. They will bring Bankruptcy and ruin upon both sections of
> the Union and will force the sacrifice of the flower of our population.
> Lincoln has shown himself utterly unworthy of his election and
> whatever may be the issue of the war his name and his party will go
> down to posterity dishonored and infamous. He assumed the right to
> subjugate us and his leading newspapers threaten us with extermina-
> tion if we do not yield to his demands. There is nothing left us there-
> fore but resistance as long as we can wield an arm.
>
> You know how earnestly I have endeavored to avert the calami-
> ties which have come upon us. But it has all been in vain. Sectional
> animosity has at last destroyed the Union and no alternative is left
> the patriot but the assertion of the rights which belong to a free
> people. When the invaders come we must meet him as we did the
> British in the Revolutionary War.
>
> Prepare yourself, my dear Daughter, for the trials to which you
> may be subjected by the folly of those Demagogues who have
> brought the present ruin upon the country.[42]

It was under these circumstances that the Civil War descended upon
Cadmus Marcellus Wilcox and Mary Emily Donelson. Although they were
not often in one another's company, as the struggle began they found
themselves deeply connected by a Tennessee heritage, marriage, mutual
exposure to European culture, West Point, and a commitment to Southern
independence.

Cadmus was obviously very fond of Mrs. Wilcox—now thirty-one
years old—and her children, and when his brother was elected to the first

Confederate Congress and had to leave his family in Texas to go off to Richmond for legislative sessions, Cadmus became his sister-in-law's solicitous, albeit intermittent, correspondent. It was an odd sort of exchange they kept up, for while he unburdened himself to her, writing freely of his most private concerns, ambitions, and disappointments, he invariably addressed her as "Sister Mary," and his letters always closed rather unfamiliarly, "Your brother, C. M. Wilcox."

CHAPTER TWO

A Strange New Army

WHEN CADMUS WILCOX CAME INTO THE CONFEDERACY, HE WAS REGARDED by the Richmond authorities, who were frantically attempting to organize an army, as a valuable asset. Not only was Wilcox one of a handful of seasoned officers they had at their disposal, but the fact that he was a professional soldier from the Regular army meant that he could be assigned to any command without consideration of which state he was from. This was no small factor in this confederated force of volunteers going to war to establish the independence of each state from the control and dictates of a central authority. Governors would reluctantly send their sons across their state line to Virginia to fight, but they would not easily tolerate their being commanded by officers from other states. Most often the undrilled and undisciplined regiments pouring chaotically into Richmond were commanded by some lawyer-politician who had raised his unit himself, campaigning for enlistments in his locale as if for office. In a sense he was, for the organizer invariably claimed the rank of colonel for the effort, however untrained he might be for the responsibility.

But the "West P'inters," as the Southern farmboys called them, could by virtue of their professionalism be placed wherever needed, and though serious resistance might be encountered for other reasons, they wouldn't be rejected solely because of their place of origin. They were looked upon as virtually stateless, a breed apart.

After Wilcox, still uncomfortable in his strange new uniform of gray, reported for assignment at the Confederate capital, Samuel Cooper, the army's white-haired adjutant and inspector general, alerted Gen. P. G. T.

Beauregard on July 26, 1861, that Wilcox had been given the temporary rank of colonel but added that both he and the officer being sent with him—another academy man named Nathaniel Evans—"can be employed in higher commands, as necessity may require."[1]

The day after he arrived in Richmond from the Southwest, Wilcox was put in charge of the 9th Alabama Regiment. Soon other Alabama units were placed under him, and it was with the troops of that state that Wilcox would be long associated. He may have been from Memphis, but not once during the entire war did he lead Tennessee troops.

The unit numbered 844 men. At his initial meeting with the Alabamians, Wilcox said, "the regiment expressed themselves well pleased at having an old army man assigned to their command."[2] Perhaps the response was a bit hasty, as the volunteers had no idea what performance standards a Regular army officer demanded of those under him.

Given his background and temperament, Wilcox could only have been aghast at the sight of the sort of soldiers he was given to direct and over-whelmed by the magnitude of the task he faced in preparing both officers and men for combat service. Clearly, discipline was going to be the fore-most challenge.

The 8th Alabama was typical of the regiments eventually entrusted to Wilcox. The atmosphere in camp fairly conveyed what the regimental officers were up against in coping with the mentality and culture of the volunteers coming into their confused ranks. This regiment was made up of companies from both the city and the country. Five companies were from Mobile, including one made up of Irishmen—the Emerald Guards—and another known as the German Fusiliers. The company from Selma, the Independent Blues, was largely composed of sons of wealthy fami-lies, though the percentage of slaveholders in the regiment was probably not more than 25 percent, according to one of the officers of the 8th Alabama. If few of the men owned slaves, that practice nevertheless influenced the general attitude toward military discipline. As one officer put it:

> The institution of slavery had created where it then existed in the United States a spirit of caste and race pride that made of every white man in some sort an aristocrat no matter whether educated or un-educated. Obedience to the commands of another—that was for the inferior race, the slave. Individual liberty, the right to do as he pleased, was the birthright of every white man born or living in the atmosphere of the South.[3]

Many of the men carried this attitude into the army, and it was clear that the officers had a tough job ahead of them. In one instance, when an affluent private of the 8th Alabama wanted to hire a buggy to ride in rather than march, his commanding officer put a quick stop to that notion. The enlisted men were outraged that their companion was denied such a privilege. "What made the matter worse was the Colonel did not even give a reason for his refusal," one observed.[4]

On another occasion, Capt. Hilary A. Herbert had to give an order to a lawyer from his hometown who was a generation older than himself. When his colonel heard him address the man as Mr. Ross, he said to the captain, "There are no 'misters' in this regiment. They are all officers, non-commissioned officers and privates. Call him Private Ross."[5]

A young officer in the 11th Alabama, Capt. John C. C. Sanders, newly graduated from the University of Alabama, initially felt that "it is very embarrassing to be ordering men to work like a parcel of negroes."[6] It didn't take Sanders long, however, to get used to exercising his authority. When some of the men, annoyed by their treatment, handed Sanders a petition calling for his resignation, he studied it carefully and then simply tore it up.[7]

One of the few officers Wilcox had under him at this time with any military training was Lt. Col. John W. Frazier, who had also been to West Point. Frazier appeared to be as exasperated as Wilcox with his men. During one drill session he cursed a volunteer captain for failing to give the correct order to his battalion and got in reply from the subaltern: "I did done it, sir, by dam, I did done it!"[8]

To a large extent, the company officers were on their own to learn their duties, and as Captain Herbert put it, "company officers were left to dig for knowledge in Hardee's Tactics and ah, how hard that was, and how slowly the knowledge came!"[9]

Some of the volunteers in Wilcox's ranks had arrived overequipped and overloaded for field service, with heavy topcoats and useless derringers. Others were woefully unprepared. Captain Sanders of the 11th Alabama said of his regiment, "Some of the companies look pretty rough, some not having any knapsacks, tents, uniforms or any camp equipage."[10]

Wilcox may well have felt somewhat overdressed for the casual sort of military organization he was joining. His troops got a glimpse of him in his new gray tunic, adorned with swirling gold Austrian knots on the sleeves, and his natty French kepi, but before long Wilcox was much more recognizable in a broad-brimmed straw hat and a short, round jacket of the sort the Mexicans favored, hickory switch in hand, astride his much-loved

Cadmus Marcellus Wilcox, nattily uniformed early in the war. LIBRARY OF CONGRESS.

white pony. In recent years, Wilcox had cultivated long, elaborate side-
burns that dangled from the side of his swarthy face. But he soon did away
with that tonsorial touch; a very short haircut, full but neat mustache, and
clean-shaven cheeks once more rendered his dark eyes, fixed and direct, the
dominant facial feature. In undergoing these changes in appearance,
Wilcox was wisely demonstrating his adaptability to the rustics in his regiments, who abhorred stiffness and formality in their officers.

The men found Colonel Wilcox a lively and sociable man, though
rather jumpy. One officer referred to Wilcox's "characteristic nervousness."11 So pronounced was his tendency to fuss about details that the

irreverent boys under him—always ready to seize upon any peculiarity to bestow a sobriquet on their officers—began calling Wilcox "Old Billy Fixin" behind his back.[12]

Wilcox had little time to get acquainted with his new command before, less than six weeks after his resignation from the U.S. Army, he was moving toward Manassas and his first encounter with blue-clad troops following the "old flag." Few of the other Regular army officers who had "gone South" had been forced to make such a hasty adjustment to their altered roles, and given the length of time Wilcox had been on the other side, the juxtapositioning must have been traumatic.

Initially, Wilcox had been assigned to a brigade made up of his 9th Alabama, the 10th and 11th Alabama, the 19th Mississippi, and the 38th Virginia regiments. The commander was Edmund Kirby Smith, who had graduated from West Point a year before Wilcox and had been a major in the 2nd U.S. Cavalry in Texas when the war broke out. At this time, the brigade was part of Gen. Joseph E. Johnston's force in the Shenandoah Valley. In the consolidation with Beauregard's troops being carried out, the unit was moving by rail to Manassas Junction when an accident kept Wilcox and his men out of the battle. A train collision ahead of the cars they were riding delayed their arrival on the field until the day after the fighting was over.

Among the Confederate wounded was Kirby Smith, who had gone to Manassas ahead of his men. When his brigade finally arrived, the men saw him pass in an ambulance. As a young lieutenant of the 11th Alabama named George Clark described it: "The brigade opened ranks and presented arms as he passed. The old fellow raised his head and saluted back, notwithstanding it could be seen that he was suffering intensely."[13]

It was the last they saw of their first brigadier. When he was healed, he was transferred elsewhere, and Clark's main recollection of the general would be of a man hardly "striking looking" who "rode a very indifferent looking old horse."[14] As yet unaware of how Kirby Smith's wounding was to affect him personally, Wilcox did not refer to it when he sat down to write in his hurried, run-together style, his first wartime letter to "Sister Mary," from "Camp on Bull Run" on August 1, 1861, covering everything from what he had seen and heard of the crushing defeat of the Federal troops to his career prospects.

It is not possible for the mind to picture a more pitiable specta-
cle than this routed army in their wild flight.

In vain did a few officers attempt to rally them they would fire
upon such of their officers as would attempt to check them in their
flight, they threw away their arms, haversacks, clothing & even
pulled off & threw away the coats on their backs in order that they
might flee the faster.

Although he had been made an infantry colonel little more than a
month before—a leap of three grades—Wilcox in the same letter revealed
that the career officer's curse of ambition had already gotten hold of him in
this new army where opportunity seemed so abundant compared with the
chances for advancement in the Regular army.

It may be that I will have good luck in this war, for I was told that
Beauregard had telegraphed Jeff Davis to make me a Brigadier General & to place me in command of five Louisiana Regiments. . . .
Now should I be a GENERAL wouldn't it be a great thing? I was
told in sober earnest that Beauregard had asked this of the President
but don't say anything about it for I may not get it & it might be
thought that I had sought it & been disappointed.[15]

A few weeks later he implored Mary Emily not to repeat to anyone
what he had said about his possible promotion. "You know to others it is
distasteful to hear a man write or to speak of himself."

He also was worried about his health. Without disclosing what malady
was afflicting him, he confided, "My health is not good but I can attend to
all my duties . . . everyone thinks I am well, but I am not, & if I should
have to live in a tent this winter I do not believe I can stand it."[16]

On October 11, 1861, while the idle army was encamped at Centreville, now training in earnest after the first battle had made that need
apparent, Wilcox indicated he still was not feeling well, as he groused, "Our
commissary is not as abundant as it should be. Although I am a colonel yet
I have not the comforts that I had in the old army as a lieutenant."[17]

One comfort he did have that he had never enjoyed as a lieutenant was a
camp servant. Though Wilcox would refer in his writings to the "blot of slavery" on the nation, it was clear that he was very much part of that system.
This is evident in his casual note to a supply officer in Richmond: "I send my
Servant Jim after my Saddle; I was much pressed for time yesterday & could
not wait for it. Will you have the kindness to deliver the Saddle to my boy."[18]

Another side of Wilcox that became plain in the handling of his routine affairs was his insistence on all he felt he had coming to him by virtue of his rank. The Confederates had adopted most of the Regular army's practices, understandably enough, including that of having officers file a form for their pay. The application included a line for years of service in order to determine a stipend. On his, Wilcox claimed fifteen years, perhaps forgetting the fact that those years were served in not this but the enemy's army.[19]

———

On October 21, 1861, Wilcox received the promotion he coveted. He was now Brig. Gen. Cadmus Wilcox, in command of Kirby Smith's brigade of Alabama, Mississippi, and Virginia troops, as well as a battery of artillery. It was difficult to imagine that four months before he had been a lowly captain in the 7th Infantry. As delighted as he was with his promotion, it would have annoyed him to learn that it might have come even sooner, for Beauregard had sought to have Wilcox assigned to him as a brigadier back in July but was informed that "Gen. Johnston says he can not spare Col. Wilcox."[20]

After his elevation, Wilcox bravely informed Mary Emily, "I will do my utmost to serve our Confederacy even to the extent of my life if it should be necessary or would contribute to our success." The same letter contained a bit of practical advice concerning his brother John, who was considering going into the army. If John did take such a step, Cadmus thought that with his background he should seek a general's commission:

> We have quite a number of Brigadier Generals from civil life who do not know a great deal and I know if your husband were a general & did not know much he could soon learn enough to make himself respected by those that did know.[21]

Family considerations aside, in the tolerant attitude toward the politician-turned-soldier that Wilcox displayed, he stood apart from most of the other West Point professionals in the army, who had nothing but disdain for the civil leaders with whom they found themselves vying for command. An academy man whom Wilcox knew well, a personable Virginian named Harry Heth, once said in disgust of the politician under whom he had to serve that he was "as incapacitated for the work he had undertaken as I would have been to lead an Italian opera."[22]

Perhaps Wilcox was being a bit more pragmatic and realized that there were not nearly enough West Pointers available to fill all the posts being created in the ever-growing army. Whoever could demonstrate a knack for shaping the material they had to work with and lead troops in battle was needed, regardless of his background or profession.

Although it would not endure, Wilcox began to have a change in attitude toward the soldiers of the United States. Maybe he was just trying to deal with conflicts over his own switch in loyalty, but in his November 18, 1861 letter to Mary Emily he confessed, "I find that I have begun to feel a little bitter against them for they have acted too badly in a great many cases, imprisoning men for no offense."[23]

Eight days later, he wrote his sister-in-law from Centreville:

> Among our prisoners are some of my old army associates but I have seen but little of them. Several of them have made eager enquiries as to Cadmus & where was he? and what is his rank? and tell him to call and see me, but I have seen nothing of them except my namesake Col. Wilcox [Orlando Willcox] of Michigan & who was with me at the Point three years & he I saw thru an accident. I do not care to see them when we have taken them in battle fighting against us on our own soil & committing the many outrages that they do.[24]

The incident to which Wilcox referred occurred at Bull Run after his old schoolmate, Col. Orlando Willcox of Detroit, was shot in the arm and made a prisoner. Cadmus was passing a church on the field that was being used as a hospital when he came upon Orlando, and he had the Union officer removed to a house in the rear and secured special attention for him. When he was healed, Wilcox exerted his influence to try to obtain an exchange for him. Such consideration for another West Pointer was only what those who really knew him would have expected from Wilcox.

Wilcox's range of army acquaintances was by this time extensive, and when Mary Emily happened to drop the names of two officers from West Point whom she had met in San Antonio, Wilcox was able to tell her offhandedly, "I like Sibley very much, McNeill is a very nice fellow but he's too fond of drink."[25] Wilcox could have met Henry H. Sibley, inventor of the Sibley tent, in Mexico or during the Seminole War. Henry C. McNeill, who graduated with the class of 1857, may have been one of the cadets Wilcox had to discipline when he was serving as commandant at the academy. Wilcox's remarks are just one more indication of how closely knit the officer corps was and how a man's standing within that fraternity could differ from the view held by the civil authorities, who couldn't have known him as well.

In the same correspondence, Wilcox, the military scholar, inquired about the books he had sent to his sister-in-law when he left Fort Fillmore and the U.S. Army. "If you ever get them, open the box at once for the books will spoil from mildew," he said. "Keep the books carefully for many of them are the very best of French military works."[26]

He certainly seemed a man consumed with his profession.

Centreville, aside from being a vast training complex for the army in Virginia, was also a place of reunion for the Southern West Pointers. There was time to renew old ties with acquaintances from the academy, Mexico, and the various frontier forts and to compare experiences in this new, decidedly different army. Occasionally there were even opportunities to meet under flags of truce with friends over in the Union lines and to pass canteens around for a cheerful swig or two before resuming preparations for the next battle against one another.

Wilcox found himself serving under Longstreet, of all people. Highly esteemed by the Confederate leadership, "Pete" had quickly become a major general in command of a huge division. For a time, no one at Centreville appeared to be enjoying the social atmosphere more than he, whether demonstrating his skill in the riding competitions or at the poker table. Aides marveled at his capacity for liquor. But he turned somber and taciturn after the sudden loss of three of his four children in a scarlet fever epidemic that swept through Richmond. Thereafter, Longstreet was a grim, serious commander, and Wilcox's relationship with him appeared quite formal and correct.

George E. Pickett, the showy Virginian of whom Longstreet was so fond (and one of Wilcox's few classmates to graduate lower than he from the academy), was another one of the brigade commanders.

How the men in the ranks perceived the professional soldiers they were being exposed to for the first time often differed from the images officers probably thought they were projecting. Young Capt. John Sanders of the 11th Alabama wrote of seeing General Beauregard when the commander stopped near his camp and was conversing with staff members:

> He is a small man, weighs about 130 or 140 lbs. looks comparatively young, wears a mustache, looks something of a "French dandy"

you can see the resemblance of the French, is getting grey, has a keen eye, eyelids look like they are about half closed. I also had the pleasure of seeing Gen. [Joseph E.] Johnston, he is an old man, grey headed, rather large, and stern looking.[27]

Having escaped the first big battle, many of Wilcox's men fell casualties instead to disease in camp during that long first winter of the war. Measles, particularly, seemed to strike the camps, and very often fatally. The soldiers from the crowded cities were seemingly more immune to the diseases that swept through the unsanitary, confined campgrounds than the rustics so much more accustomed to the outdoors, clean air, and limited exposure to strangers. Observed young Lt. George Clark, "Remarkable as it may seem, the stout country boys whom it may be supposed could stand all kinds of hardships, were the first to succumb, while the city boys as a rule escaped."

Even when the brigade moved its campsite four miles away to Bristoe Station, disease followed. "Here we remained in camp for fully two months and during a greater portion of the time most of the men were sick, the well ones being required to wait on the sick ones," Clark said.[28]

A surgeon with the 11th Alabama, W. H. Sanders, gave an indication of how extensive the epidemic was when he wrote on August 19 after losing another man:

This makes nine patients we have had to die in camp, a number which appears frightful at first but when we remember that during the two months we have had not less than eight hundred cases of sickness—four hundred of which have been measles, this number is perhaps as small as it could be in the ordinary course of events.[29]

Wilcox had never seen such an outbreak of diseases in camp. "We have had an incredible amount of sickness," he wrote Mary Emily. In his old 9th Alabama, Wilcox said there were "more than 300 sick at one time & in other regiments it has been even worse. . . . I have had about 25 deaths."[30]

The winter of idleness and sickness was tough to endure, and much of the volunteers' ardor for military life dissipated. Stern discipline was required to keep the men in line, and being under the command of a rough Regular army officer like Wilcox did not enhance morale among his increasingly miserable troops. A member of the Thomas Artillery wrote to his family in Richmond that December that the general was "a very wicked and unpopular man."[31]

When spring finally came, Wilcox's men were relieved to vacate the wretched, infectious campgrounds around Centreville as the war was transferred to a different theater. George B. McClellan was now the commander of the Army of the Potomac and was attempting in his methodical way to advance up the Peninsula between the York and James Rivers directly on Richmond. Outnumbered, the Confederates were slowly retreating, backing up closer and closer to their capital. Again, Wilcox's command was late to the fray, but it was not its own fault. The brigade had first been sent by rail all the way to Weldon, North Carolina, a locale thought threatened, and then was summoned back to the Peninsula, traveling first by train and then on a flotilla of boats down the James River, disembarking at King's Landing.

The makeup of the unit Wilcox was leading into battle so circuitously had been altered somewhat. The 8th Alabama regiment had been added and the Virginia and Mississippi regiments transferred, leaving Wilcox with an all-Alabama brigade of four regiments—the sort of homogeneous composition both officers and men preferred.

The Confederate general in charge of the Yorktown sector, Wilcox learned on his arrival, was his old friend from Mexico and the Aztec Club, John Bankhead Magruder. A flamboyant, colorful character, Magruder carried the nickname "Prince John." Though he made an impressively regal appearance with his fine uniforms and bearing, Wilcox questioned whether there was enough substance to the man to be worthy of the responsibility given him, and he wrote to his brother John, "I would feel better satisfied if Joe Johnston was our commander, tho do not wish to disparage Magruder."[32]

The first exposure of Wilcox's boys to combat came as the army was withdrawing from Yorktown, and in a setting that should have dispelled any romantic visions of what a field of battle might be like. A heavy, unremitting rain was falling as the army struggled to get through the already marshy area in the vicinity of the old Colonial capital of Williamsburg on May 5, 1862. The men were sinking above their knees in the quagmire, cursing as they slogged along. For wagons and artillery, the mud made what roads there were virtually impassable. In the rear, units could move just a few yards at a time before the lurching procession in front of them backed up. And the Federals, stubbornly determined to follow the swampy route all the way to Richmond, were always close behind.

Orders came for Wilcox to occupy a hastily constructed series of redoubts and report to Gen. Richard H. Anderson, a South Carolinian who had been four years ahead of Wilcox at the academy and a former captain of dragoons. It looked as if Wilcox's first fight was to be a rear-guard delaying action, but after joining Anderson, he learned that Longstreet had other plans. With Pickett's brigade in support, Anderson's command was ordered to leave its works and attack. In Wilcox's sector, this meant first crossing an open field and encountering an enemy battery in deep woods, "so dense that a colonel could not see his entire regiment when in line of battle." Beyond the patch of woods, behind a rail fence, was a Union line of about three brigades. After sending for reinforcements for his brigade, which, due to the absence of some units, was down to just 1,100 men, Wilcox started forward, and his troops were soon engaged in a close musketry fight. Gradually the Yanks gave ground, backing up through an area where a mass of full-grown pine trees had recently been cut, the logs, branches, and brush providing thick cover for the troops falling back and disrupting the advancing Rebel line.[33]

The attacking Confederates learned quickly how to replenish their ammunition in a fight. Wilcox noted with satisfaction: "After the enemy had been driven into the fallen timber this regiment as well as others refilled their cartridge boxes from those of the enemy's dead. Their knapsacks contained 60 rounds."[34]

The fighting continued until the Federals were driven over the Yorktown Road and into another thicket. Finally, night ended the contest. The brigade had been engaged since 9 A.M. in the delaying action, did not leave the field until 11 P.M., and by 2 A.M. was back in line resuming the retreat toward Richmond. In this, what Wilcox called "their first collision with the enemy," his brigade had not only helped drive back and scatter the army's pursuers, but also captured a battery of six rifled pieces. His casualties had been 161 men, including 25 dead.[35] In his report, Longstreet called Williamsburg "a very handsome affair" and stated "my part in the battle was comparatively simple and easy, that of placing the troops in proper positions at proper times"—the very things that he did so superbly.[36] There was not a general in the army, it would seem, who could handle large numbers of troops on a battlefield as effortlessly and unflappably as Longstreet. As one staff officer put it, "He was like a rock in steadiness when sometimes in battle the world seemed flying to pieces."[37]

Young Lt. George Clark of the 11th Alabama could attest to the bulky general's calming influence in combat. He described one scene during the campaign:

> The cannon shots plowed up the turnpike, and in the midst of
> it, down walked General Longstreet. He was on foot with his sword

Lt. Gen. James Longstreet, with whom Wilcox was often at odds.
LIBRARY OF CONGRESS.

across the back of his neck, notwithstanding the cannon balls were flying all around him, and stopped to talk with us. He seemed as passive as if he were in his own home.[38]

In distributing praise, Longstreet said in his report on Williamsburg that "the brigades of Generals C. M. Wilcox and A. P Hill were long and hotly engaged. Ably led by those commanders, they drove the enemy from every position." Even after the fighting was over, Longstreet said Wilcox's was one of the brigades that deserved credit "for the good order of their march during the night and the following day."[39]

Wilcox couldn't have asked more of Longstreet by way of recognition of his work under the most difficult of conditions. But this relationship would soon change.

Though it was still early in the war, Wilcox was already demonstrating an unattractive trait that would become progressively more pronounced—a tendency to believe that whenever someone was advanced ahead of him, merit had nothing to do with it, only some unfair advantage that had been exercised. He came away from Williamsburg convinced that A. P. Hill—an outstanding, inspiring combat leader with whom he was well acquainted—was made a major general on the basis of his having been wrongly credited with the capture of the Union battery that had, in fact, been taken by Wilcox's own 9th Alabama Regiment. It was an absurd supposition, but Wilcox's ego seemed to demand that one of his peers could not have inched ahead of him on ability alone.

Less than four weeks later came what was called the battle of Seven Pines, in which Wilcox found himself in command of three full brigades—his own, the Mississippi brigade of Winfield Scott Featherston (the man whose seat in Congress had been captured by Wilcox's brother back in 1851), and the Virginia unit commanded by thirty-four-year-old Roger A. Pryor, a lawyer turned newspaper editor (and rather notorious duelist) who had given up a seat in the Confederate Congress to enter the army. Considering the backgrounds of Featherston and Pryor, it is not surprising that their brigades were placed under the more experienced hand of someone like Wilcox at this critical moment, and the three were closely associated for some time.

The action began promisingly enough for Wilcox, but a series of countermanded orders from Longstreet soon had him bewildered and vexed. Given Longstreet's acknowledged skill at maneuvering troops in the field under the most confused circumstances, his contradictory actions at Seven Pines were no doubt excusable and could be looked upon as responses to developments. But Wilcox had no view of the broader situation as his men splashed through the miserable bog they were sent into.

First Wilcox was ordered to move up the Charles City Road in rear of Benjamin Huger's division, and then he was told to precede Huger's. No sooner had he passed Huger's brigades than he was directed to counter-march to the Williamsburg Road. After retracing their steps for a mile, orders came again from Longstreet to about-face and march down the Charles City Road. As Wilcox later wrote:

> Again orders were received in writing to move across to the Williamsburg road, following country roads and paths through woods and fields, a guide being furnished to conduct the command. The intervening distance between the two roads was low and flat, and in many places covered with water and at one point waist-deep. The march was of necessity very slow.[40]

After an exhausting, frustrating day, Wilcox at 10 P.M. was instructed to move farther to the front and relieve another brigade. The night was intensely dark, and as the troops sloshed ahead, they heard the cries of the enemy's wounded in the woods and swamps on their left and right. After the men had had little or no sleep, the fighting resumed at dawn.[41]

"The engagement, now raging furiously, was going on as well as could be desired," Wilcox wrote, "but just at this time an order in writing was sent to me to withdraw my command, which was instantly done."[42]

If he had made a simple recitation in his report of how roughly his brigades had been used by his superiors in the torturous marsh in which the army was operating, Wilcox's plight probably would have been readily appreciated by the high command. But he made the mistake of adding a postscript to his official report that was bound to get him in trouble:

> P.S.—When the head of my column reached the Williamsburg road Longstreet said, "You have taken a good deal of time to reach this road;" for that reason I reported the orders and counter-orders, marches and counter-marches he had given, and that I had made in obedience to his orders.

Wilcox closed the addendum with two uncalled-for observations that no doubt would have further infuriated the vain Longstreet if he got wind of them. "Seven Pines, the successful part of it, was D. H. Hill's fight. I have thought that General Huger was a little too much censured for Seven Pines by the papers."[43]

How much Longstreet learned of what Wilcox had written is unclear, but his regard for Wilcox as a soldier was forever diminished by his performance at Seven Pines. However unjustified his criticism may have been, given the abominable conditions on the field, Longstreet henceforth never missed an opportunity to show his contempt. Longstreet wrote much later that he had asked "Jeb" Stuart if there were obstacles impeding Wilcox's marching route, and "he reported that there was nothing more than swamp lands, hardly knee-deep."[44]

An arbitrator might have found a convincing witness in Lieutenant Clark of the 11th Alabama, who wrote:

> The mud was very deep, as the country was almost a swamp. . . . I remember in going back to Richmond in the dark, that I stepped into quicksand and sank to my shoulder. It was fortunate for me that two or three of my boys got hold of me in time to pull me out before I sank any further.[45]

Wilcox later wrote rather amusingly of what a discovery this part of the state had been, both for himself and for many other Southerners: "The ground over which our last battle was fought was low, wet and swampy. I had no idea that there was so much low ground in Virginia and so near Richmond."[46]

The rift between the two men—one that would become irreparable when Longstreet began to openly champion his friend Pickett for a division command over Wilcox—was by no means unusual in this army. It merely underscored the fact that these professional officers who had gone with the Confederacy harbored emotions that sometimes became far stronger than the devotion and dedication they felt for the cause. Jealousy, ambition, and spite could be found at the root of many of these schisms. Often the personal conflict could be traced back decades to incidents that had occurred at the military academy.

Some of these men were consumed by vanity, and at times they let imagined slights influence their command decisions, even with fighting men's lives at stake. When a competent officer's standing was deliberately undermined by a rival's planting of inaccurate accounts of engagements in influential newspapers or ignoring the exploits of another in official reports to restrict his advancement, the army's entire command structure was weakened.

Such feuds were so common that it is hard to believe that all these generals were on the same side. While Wilcox was seething over the incidents with Longstreet, A. P. Hill could barely contain his explosive temper in dealing with the cold, aloof "Stonewall" Jackson, who had been his classmate at West Point. And the West Point tie didn't prevent one of Wilcox's former students there, John S. Marmaduke (class of 1857), from going out and shooting Gen. L. M. Walker (class of 1850) to death in a duel resulting from an accusation of cowardice made against Walker.

Superiors placed subordinates under arrest on the most trivial or baseless charges with such frequency that officers were spending as much time preparing court-martial defenses as they were on all their other administrative responsibilities. Cadmus Wilcox's own quarrels could be looked upon as typical of the testy officer corps in which he served.

An infinitely more significant outcome of the battle of Seven Pines as far as leadership was concerned was the replacement of the wounded Joseph E. Johnston with Gen. Robert E. Lee as commander of the army.

To the professional officer corps, there was an inevitability about the emergence of Lee. When they looked around them and saw the organizational structure this new army was taking, the question all these career soldiers who had known him in Mexico, at the military academy, in Texas, or in some other place of duty could only ask was, where is Lee? Now fifty-five years old, the revered Virginian had been serving obscurely as a military adviser to President Davis and to date had had little active involvement in the war. When he finally gained command of the army, however, it surprised no one; it was only, as Wilcox himself indicated, what was anticipated by those who knew him.

Wilcox could only have counted Lee's appointment as another sign that he might "have good luck in this war" because, if anyone, Lee was aware through long association what a dutiful officer he had been. One wonders if Wilcox's extraordinary report on Seven Pines, dated more than a week after Lee took command, was not worded specifically to make certain that Lee understood what Wilcox had been up against in that engagement. But if so, the attempt may have backfired by leaving Lee with the impression that Wilcox was having trouble with the man on whom Lee must greatly rely—Longstreet. It was a conflict that he must be careful not to exacerbate by, in his relations with Wilcox, offending Longstreet.

Still, if Wilcox felt himself in luck, it was because he was also aware of his family ties to Lee. His younger brother, Robert, was to be placed on special assignment for a time at Lee's headquarters. Another family connection with Lee stemmed from the fact that Mary Emily Wilcox's sixty-one-year-old uncle, Daniel S. Donelson, had served under him during the abortive West Virginia campaign in 1861 as a brigadier in command of a Tennessee and a Georgia regiment. Subsequently, the old West Pointer who had become a planter (and after whom the fort he had built for the Confederacy on the Cumberland River had been named) had been sent with his command to the South Carolina coast to again report to Lee, who was improving defenses there.

On June 8, 1862, Wilcox was able to write to Mary Emily: "Your old friend General Lee is now in command of the army since the wounding of Gen. Johnston. . . . I have every confidence in him for I know that he is both brave & prudent."[47]

Lee had been a guest at Mrs. Wilcox's christening three decades back, and presumably his contacts with the Donelsons continued over the ensuing years. When, in 1857, Lee came to San Antonio to replace Albert Sidney Johnston in command of the 2nd Cavalry, when Johnston was summoned to Washington to lead an expedition against the defiant Mormons in Utah, they surely would have met again socially. Mary Emily's eventful life had brought her in touch with many persons of prominence, and she must have been pleased to learn that her ambitious brother-in-law was serving under a man she had so much admired (and whose opinion of her adopted state as "a desert of dullness" the sophisticated lady may well have shared). She may also have wished that her younger brother, John Samuel Donelson, who had graduated from Yale in 1854, was with Lee also rather than serving with Gen. Preston Smith's brigade in the West.

But neither Wilcox nor anyone else could ever know for certain where he stood with Lee, who was so reserved and undemonstrative in manner. Wilcox did know that with this commanding general nothing was considered more important that simply doing one's duty.

―――――⟫⊕⟪―――――

The battles of the Seven Days were fought with the steeples of Richmond's churches often visible in the Confederates' rear, so dangerously close had the fall of their capital become. Never again would the army be involved in such ferocious fighting on a sustained basis as was experienced during that dreadful, exhausting, nerve-straining, desperate week that followed Lee's assumption of command. When the threat was finally lifted, names such as Gaines' Mill, Frayser's Farm, Mechanicsville, Savage Station, and Malvern

Gen. Robert E. Lee, with whom Wilcox was so closely associated throughout his career.
VALENTINE MUSEUM

Hill were being sewn on battle flags by various regiments to show on how many of those days of horrific warfare they had been sent into combat. It was the severest test to which the Confederate combat leaders had been placed, and few withstood the ordeal as well as Cadmus Wilcox.

Fighting on difficult ground under the most confused conditions, Wilcox not only had held responsibility for his own Alabama brigade, but also once more was placed in charge of the brigades of the inexperienced Featherston and Pryor. Not many units sustained the shocking losses Wilcox endured, and he did so without hesitation or apology. It was the price that had to be paid for developing a command such as the Alabama brigade that would close with the enemy to a point where it could do damage. His was not going to be one of those units that stood back and fired from distances where it could neither inflict nor sustain serious casualties, only generate a good deal of smoke and noise. But how long could Wilcox continue to take such losses?

At Gaines' Mill, to get his troops into position to attack, he had first to somehow get across a deep ravine through which ran Beaver Dam Creek. General Featherston had already expressed the view that the creek was impassable. "General Wilcox, who was close by and heard the report, with his characteristic nervousness said to General Longstreet, 'My people can cross it,'" one of his colonels recalled.[48]

After bringing up a battery to disperse the Union soldiers in rifle pits and behind trees on the opposite slope, his engineers found the supporting beams for a destroyed bridge by the stream, and collecting some planks from an abandoned enemy bivouac, they erected a serviceable if rickety span in half an hour for infantry and artillery to cross.

Working his way into position in front of the left of the Union line, Wilcox said, "I now made my preparations for an attack upon the enemy, intending it to be made with the utmost vigor and with all the force at my command."[49] That clearly was his style. The forming of his attacking lines took place under what he liked to call a "brisk" enfilading fire of artillery from the enemy's batteries of rifled cannon from the heights beyond the Chickahominy. When he was satisfied with their alignment, Wilcox permitted his troops to advance from under the artillery fire to which they were being subjected up a slope atop which they knew they would encounter the Federals' main line. When they reached the crest and came in full view of the Union troops, his men, according to Wilcox, "were instantly met by a heavy and destructive fire of infantry within less than 100 yards."[50]

The Rebels faced two lines of breastworks, one above the other on some rising ground in front of them, while still another row of bluecoats was using a small streambed in front of them as a rifle pit. From somewhere in the rear of the enemy infantry, unseen batteries raked them with solid shot, grape, and canister.

"Our men still press on with unabated fury," Wilcox recounted, until the Union soldiers, shaken, began to yield. "Our loss has been up to this time severe, but now the enemy is made to suffer," the brigadier observed. "No longer screened by his breastworks or standing timber, his slaughter is terrible. Our men have no difficulty in chasing him before them in every and all directions." The Yanks were driven to the swamp of the Chickahominy, and the pursuit was "only arrested by night."[51]

Whether or not the first crack in the Union line at Gaines' Mill had come in Wilcox's sector, his breakthrough contributed to the general collapse of the position. When the casualties were tallied, it was found that in just the Alabama brigade, there were 584 killed, wounded, and missing. And this from a force of about 1,850 men. "In driving the enemy from this strong position our loss was heavy, but we should be profoundly grateful that it was not more so," wrote Wilcox.[52]

Among the wounded was young Lieutenant Clark of the 11th Alabama, who found himself particularly well taken care of. He had been struck in the arm and was sitting on a log at a dressing station, bleeding heavily and waiting to be treated, when a Catholic priest approached him and closed the wound himself, explaining to Clark that he had gained experience in such things in European wars. In addition to a bandage, the priest gave the youth a bottle of brandy.

"I need not say that I availed myself of this," Clark related. "My negro boy and I went down by a large tree, no one being around. He made me a pallet, and he and I began the task of drinking up that bottle of brandy."[53]

Wilcox had come close to personally adding to the casualty list. Seeing one of his men standing on an elevation beneath a tree, he called up to him to ask if he could see the Union troops from there. When the soldier said that he could, Wilcox climbed up to join him. As he arrived at the top, a cannonball shattered the tree above him, and the general scampered down again.

"Did you get a good view?" the private asked his commander.

"Too good for me," Wilcox replied and rode on. He was not a young lieutenant anymore and this was not the Belen gate at Chapultepec to brave. He was a thirty-eight-year-old brigadier now and such foolhardy heroics were behind him.[54]

If he had been annoyed by Wilcox's slowness at Seven Pines, Longstreet was ready to give him full credit for his work at Gaines' Mill. "There was more individual gallantry displayed upon this field than any I have every seen," Longstreet reported, adding that C. M. Wilcox was conspicuous.

But Wilcox's part in the Seven Days wasn't over. Two days later, the fighting shifted to Frayser's Farm.[55] Though the action for Wilcox's unit did not get under way until 6 P.M., in the little daylight remaining he was involved in some of the most intense combat his men would encounter.

Wilcox, an officer who liked to study carefully the terrain in which he was to operate, was in the awkward position of having no knowledge of the topography over which he was ordered to march that day.

When he approached a stretch of woods so thick that his command couldn't advance in line of battle, he drew on his experience in maneuvering troops to order his regiments to march by the right flank in narrow formation.

After crossing an open field, his regiments swept over and captured two six-gun batteries that had been perforating the Confederate lines with grape and canister. The struggle for the guns came down to personal duels, and many soldiers received bayonet wounds. One of his lieutenants, Wilcox observed, "had a hand-to-hand collision with an officer, and having just dealt a severe blow upon his adversary he fell, cut over the head with a saber-bayonet from behind, and had afterward three bayonet wounds in the face and two in the breast." All four of the colonels in the brigade were also wounded.

The Union troops were driven into the woods, but they soon re-formed and came back at Wilcox's men for a second close-quarters fight. This time the Southerners, with no support coming up, had to give ground. They relinquished one of their captured batteries and retired to some pine woods, where they remained until sunset, when, with ammunition exhausted, they were withdrawn and replaced with fresh troops.

At the end of the day, Wilcox counted six holes in his uniform, but amazingly, he had not been wounded. And he never would be, extraordinary in an army in which even general officers were expected to provide close direction in combat and, as a consequence, suffered a staggering mortality rate. The number of high-ranking officers with empty sleeves, facial scars, and limps soon became so large that it was the unmarked general who was conspicuous.

Frayser's Farm cost Wilcox another 471 killed, wounded, and missing. During the entire Seven Days battles, Wilcox had lost 1,055 men—more than half his brigade, and the highest figure of any brigade under Longstreet's command.[56]

In August, Lee—having secured the Confederate seat of government and forced the replacement, in effect, of the failed McClellan by a new adversary, the bombastic John Pope—took the offensive and launched his first movement into Maryland.

Wilcox, still in command of three brigades—his own, Pryor's, and Featherston's—had a minor skirmish at Kelly's Ford on the Rappahannock as the advance got under way. The incident merited only a brief report, but it was more revealing about the attitude toward war of this seasoned professional soldier than any of his exhaustively long accounts of his actions. After observing the work of the Thomas Artillery as the battery fired from some high ground on an enemy line crossing an open field, Wilcox wrote:

It has never been my pleasure to witness such beautiful shots as the first half dozen shells that were thrown at them. Each shell burst at the right place and time, and seemed to create more confusion and inflict greater loss upon them than the infantry fire.[57]

Wilcox experienced another harrowing escape in the affair, one that could have done nothing to calm his manner. He was riding in advance of his command when the single aide accompanying him spotted a Yankee picket behind a boulder ahead of them. When the escort asked Wilcox if he should fire, he replied in the negative; the distance was too great and it would be a waste of ammunition. Hardly were the words out of his mouth before a minié ball came whizzing within inches of the general's ear and whacked against the bank behind him.[58]

Later in the day an inaccurate report circulated that Wilcox had been wounded in the arm. Wilcox would write late in the war, "I have been reported wounded several times but have never been hurt," and cautioned his family not to believe everything the papers reported after battles. He would remain one of the few Confederate combat leaders somehow able to escape a disabling wound.[59]

Wilcox demonstrated he had not lost all sentiment for his adversaries in blue when he wrote to sister Mary about "a little incident" at Second Manassas where Pope was routed and Lee's invading army was able to move on to the Potomac.

As he was galloping across the field, Wilcox saw a white handkerchief waved at him by a wounded Union officer lying on the ground. When he stopped and dismounted, the Federal said weakly, "I am Chamberlain. I graduated at the Point while you were an instructor."

Wilcox wanted to have the man removed into a nearby ravine for safety but Chamberlain insisted that as he was mortally wounded it was not worth the risk. With artillery fire falling about them, the officer again told him not to linger, but Wilcox refused to leave his former student unattended. A battle may be raging, but he had a duty to perform that was more compelling: it was a matter of honor that a West Point man couldn't ignore.[60]

Wilcox did well at Second Manassas in the pursuit of the broken enemy forces and once more was duly recognized by Longstreet, but again his biting criticism was incorporated in an official report. This time the object was one of the brigadiers under him, Featherston, the Mississippi politician-turned-soldier and, oddly enough, one of Wilcox's strongest boosters. Wilcox wrote that he had "ordered General Featherston to move his brigade by the flank rapidly down the slope in his front, and thus take in rear or intercept the retreat of the enemy that were so closely engaged with Jackson. This order was repeated three times and in the most positive and peremptory manner, but it was not obeyed." Though it is not known whether it was because of this report, Featherston was soon gone from the Army of Northern Virginia, transferred to Vicksburg.[61]

By the time Lee's exhausted army assembled at Sharpsburg to engage in what was to be the bloodiest single day's fighting of the war, by Antietam Creek, it was down to only 35,000 men. Tens of thousands more had straggled, most of them footsore or suffering so severely from dysentery and other ailments that they could not go on. Cadmus Wilcox was among those disabled by illness, and before the battle was fought, he had to relinquish command of his brigade to the senior colonel. This was the only major battle of the war in the east at which Wilcox was not present for duty.

His presence was sorely missed. When division commander Richard Anderson was badly wounded while his division was advancing through the cornfield and orchard of the Piper farm in back of the Sunken Road, his command all but disintegrated, with no one available to exercise effective control. In the confusion, the division suffered the highest casualties of Longstreet's corps in the battle, while accomplishing next to nothing. Had Wilcox been there, command of the division would have fallen to him as the senior brigadier, and the unit would have had the benefit of his tactical knowledge and experience. It was a costly way to demonstrate Wilcox's value.

CHAPTER THREE

Ambition and Discouragement

WHEN THE ARMY STAGGERED BACK TO VIRGINIA AFTER ITS COSTLY DRAWN battle with the Army of the Potomac, Wilcox was ready to rejoin his command. He had been absent for seven or eight days, suffering most likely from severe dysentery. Almost immediately, he learned that as the ranking officer, he must take command of Anderson's division in place of its regular commander, who would be rendered *hors de combat* for months.

Wilcox soon had to comply with an odd directive from his corps commander, Longstreet. The troops were in dreadful condition after the arduous Maryland campaign. Not only were the ranks depleted by battle casualties and sickness, but those present for duty were sorely in need of shoes and other clothing. Longstreet's problem was that he had a number of English dignitaries visiting his headquarters who wanted to have a look at his regiments in formation. The delegation included Col. Garnet Wolseley of the British Army. Longstreet was no doubt aware that the chances of foreign recognition of the Confederacy might be diminished if reports were circulated abroad of the woeful state of the Rebel forces, so he decided a bit of theatrics were in order and cast Wilcox in the leading role. He notified Wilcox on October 12, 1862 that he and the British party would be reviewing Wilcox's division on the next day and the corps commander made it clear that he wanted the men to present as fine an appearance as possible. He ordered Wilcox to organize the division "into four good brigades, composed of the best drilled and clothed men," and directed another division commander, George Pickett, to provide "one full brigade of his best troops" to be reviewed as a portion of Wilcox's command.[1]

It was no simple shuffling act Wilcox had to perform overnight to present what would pass by European standards for a full-strength, fully equipped infantry division but he did his best to bring off the deception.

Cadmus's brother, now the Hon. John A. Wilcox, was a member of the House Military Affairs Committee, and General Wilcox had begun about this time to advise him on army business, unabashedly attempting to stir the congressman to use his influence to address the soldiers' needs and sometimes, it would seem, his own.

"I wish to impress on you the urgent necessity for prompt action on the part of Congress in certain matters connected with the army," Cadmus wrote John on September 26, 1862, from Martinsburg, Virginia.

"Our men are sadly in want of clothing especially shoes, many of our poor men have not changed their clothes since they left Richmond . . . 5,000 are about useless from the want of shoes."

In the same letter, the often blunt brigadier let loose probably the most critical observations on the behaviour of the soldiers of the Army of Northern Virginia one of its officers would ever deliver, a criticism that even his brother must have found startling.

"We have no discipline in our army," the general stated flatly. "It is but little better than an armed mob, the wanton destruction of private property by our army is a shame . . . where our army marches & camps desolation follows, they burn fences, pillage orchards, steal the green corn, kill beef, sheep, hogs & poultry, not in the presence of officers always but the marauding stragglers who leave their companies without authority but not to desert but come back voluntarily after being absent for a few days but many go off & remain for weeks & some never do come back but go to their homes."[2]

Perhaps Cadmus was just showing the exasperation of a Regular army officer accustomed to more rigid standards, but the politician in his brother told him that this was no letter to be shared with his colleagues promoting a much different image of the boys serving the cause.

On a personal level, Wilcox was greatly disturbed that he was not being advanced more quickly in an army where men were moving from major to major general in a matter of a few months. Wilcox had been a brigadier for a year now and might have been content to remain at that lofty rank for the remainder of his career had it not been for the way he saw others being promoted. He had served creditably in some of the fiercest engagements of the war, often being called upon to manage several brigades at a time. Yet two of his former classmates at the academy—Jackson and, of all people, Pickett, who was dead last in his class—were already major generals. A. P. Hill, the Virginian who graduated a year after him, was also a major general now in command of the renowned Light Division.

But worst of all for a career soldier such as Wilcox, who knew the other officers' length of time in grade as well as he knew their names, was the humiliation of seeing so many former students of his at the academy from 1852 to 1857 actually passing him—the man who had instructed them in basic infantry tactics—in rank. Cadet J. E. B. Stuart was now a major general in command of Lee's cavalry. John Bell Hood was a major general leading a famous infantry division. And both were almost a decade younger than Wilcox.

Wilcox could probably abide having the inexperienced, unschooled political generals placed in positions of authority in the army. He was a practical man and could recognize the necessity of sometimes accommodating men of power and influence in the civil sector as part of the give and take of government work. That was politics. What a man of his background could not endure was a loss of status among the professional soldiers with whom he had been associated. The situation gnawed at him until November 1862, when he told General Lee he wanted to leave the Army of Northern Virginia to seek better opportunities elsewhere.

Lee, a man to whom duty was all-important whether or not its performance brought promotion and recognition, responded that he was pained to learn this. "I cannot consent to it for I require your services here. You must come and see me and tell me what is the matter. I know you are too good a soldier not to serve where it is necessary for the benefit of the Confederacy."[3]

While Wilcox was making his discontent known to the commanding general, others were going around Lee to plead for his promotion in the halls of government in Richmond. In an extraordinary gesture, Brigadier General Featherston, Col. Carnot Posey, and other officers from Mississippi sent a petition on December 3, 1862, to Secretary of War James A. Seddon stating:

> The undersigned have for some months past been associated in the service in the same Division with Brig. Gen'l C. M. Wilcox. During a considerable part of this time, Gen'l Wilcox has been in command of the Division. We have had good opportunities for judging his capacity, qualifications & bearing as an officer. We, therefore,

most cheerfully bear testimony to his ability, gallantry, skill, activity, industry & energy as a commander. We have been with him in battle, on the march & in camp & most cordially recommend him to your favourable consideration for promotion.[4]

In February 1863, President Jefferson Davis had before him a petition from no fewer than fifteen congressmen calling for Wilcox's promotion. "He is spoken of and complimented in the highest terms in every report," the elected officials pointed out and argued that others "not so prominent have been promoted over him." After citing Wilcox's service in Mexico and chronicling the Civil War battles in which he had performed well, the congressmen said they considered him "among the first commanders in our army" and one who had earned promotion "to the fullest extent."[5]

It is difficult to believe that this was taking place without Wilcox's knowledge and encouragement. His brother John likely had a hand in the procurement of all those signatures in the House.

The feeling that Wilcox was being unfairly passed over must have been widespread, for Col. John C. C. Sanders of the 11th Alabama even commented on the situation to his parents in a February 10 letter: "We are and have been for some time awaiting to see Gen. Wilcox promoted to a Major Generalship. Think he deserves it, several junior officers have been promoted over him, we cannot understand why he should be neglected."[6]

In March 1863, the army rumor mill had it that Wilcox was to be given the major general's slot vacated by D. H. Hill, who had been transferred. The prospect infuriated Robert E. Rodes, a Virginia Military Institute graduate then serving in temporary command of Hill's division.

"As he [Wilcox] is a West Point man he will beat me almost to a certainty," Rodes wrote to his friend, Richard S. Ewell. "I would prefer being beaten by a baboon but will submit to it quietly, unless they place [him] in command of this Div."[7]

Was Rodes's remark meant as a slur toward military academy graduates in general or Wilcox in particular? It is difficult to imagine how Rodes might have formed such a low opinion of Wilcox. Aside from the fact that both commanded Alabama troops in the army, there seems to have been little reason for them to have come into contact with one another. At any rate, Rodes need not have been concerned; he got the promotion, making him the only infantry division commander in Lee's army who was not a U.S. Military Academy graduate.

At a time when Wilcox was so hungrily coveting promotion to major general, he was shocked to learn that Mary Emily's uncle Daniel had been given that honor by the War Department on April 22, 1863. Wilcox's surprise was not because Gen. Daniel S. Donelson's service under Braxton Bragg and then as head of the Department of East Tennessee had not been outstanding, but because Donelson had died five days before the promotion was announced.

———— ——

At about the same time, Andrew J. Donelson, back in Memphis, was exhibiting rather perplexing behavior in regard to where he stood on the war effort. At one point, he had been writing Mary Emily:

> We have no alternative but to establish our independence. If Lincoln were now to succeed the South would be ruined. He justifies measures that are at war with all our ideas of a constitutional government. He must therefore be whipped and I hope that all my friends will help do it.[8]

By the spring of 1863, however, with his Tennessee plantation behind the Union lines, he wrote the local Federal commander for permission to inspect his property: "As you are aware that I was a long time in the service of the United States, and a great portion of my life was spent in the family of Gen. Jackson whose doctrines and opinions on the subject of secession I have never abandoned."[9] Andrew Donelson's civil war, it seemed, was being fought mainly within himself.

———— ——

With his transfer request denied, Wilcox could only wait for another chance to distinguish himself. That opportunity would not come until May 1863. His sector had been almost ignored during the battle of Fredericksburg in December, and there were no other engagements of consequence during the long winter.

In February, Wilcox was in Richmond on an unorthodox recruiting mission that the duty-conscious officer may well have proposed himself. As a War Department functionary noted in his diary, "General Wilcox is organizing an impromptu brigade here formed of the furloughed officers and men found everywhere in the streets and at the hotels." Cadmus and his brother John may have been annoyed at the number of idle men in uniform that they saw loitering about and decided that a roundup might be productive, though there is no indication of how successful the recruiting effort was or how many saloon warriors were brought into his ranks.[10]

If he was also doing some politicking at the capital, Wilcox did not mention that or his press gang activity in a letter to Mary Emily about his visit. His brief note simply mentioned that he had had his photograph taken in Richmond and, if sent a copy, she would have seen a short-haired, smooth-cheeked Cadmus with a full mustache and in the plainest of gray tunics. The note closed with the admonition, "You must not let those little ones of yours forget their Uncle Cad."[11]

The two seasonally inactive armies had taken up positions on opposite sides of the Rappahannock, and the point assigned Wilcox to guard during the long winter was Bank's Ford, located three miles above Fredericksburg, one of the few crossing points the Yankees could use and therefore of vital importance. With Maj. Gen. "Dick" Anderson healed from his Antietam wounds and able to resume command of his division, Wilcox was now back with his Alabama brigade.

The 14th Alabama had by this time been transferred to Wilcox, and his brigade now comprised five full regiments—the 8th, 9th, 10th, 11th, and 14th Alabama—making it one of the strongest, most battle-tested combat units in the army.

What bothered Wilcox a great deal was the conduct of the Federal troops toward civilians and personal property in Virginia, and his anger showed in a letter to Mary Emily from Fredericksburg: "Our enemies seem to be maddened with hate . . . and goaded by the most vindictive & fiendish spirits. Seem bent on our total destruction of subjugation. . . . I did not know that any people could be so brutal." He closed by saying, "There can be no doubt as to our success for our cause is just."[12]

About the most serious administrative problem Wilcox had to contend with during this dreary stretch was that a growing number of his men were "running the blockade," slipping off at night to go down to Fredericksburg for whiskey.

The soldiers of the two armies made the narrow river dividing them something of a social and recreation center and tended to congregate along its banks, confident that they would not be molested by their enemies while warfare was informally suspended for the season.

John Piney Oden of Selma, Alabama, a forty-year-old captain in the 10th Alabama, observed one morning that his men were "very lively fixing up fish hooks, etc., preparatory for going on picket." He also noted: "The Yankees are all along on the opposite side seemingly diligent. Our heights enable one to view their forces for some distance. There is a good large force in sight. Our boys ar scattered all over the battlefield like so many cattle or sheep gathering wild onions, others are to be found up to their necks seining for fish just below a dam across the river."[13]

As one uneventful tour of guard duty followed another, Wilcox's bored pickets began to socialize with their counterparts on the other side, despite their brigade commander's animosity toward any bluecoat who was not a professional soldier. Conversation graduated to trading for scarce items aboard miniature "merchant vessels" the sentries sailed back and forth, with coffee, sugar, and tobacco the most popular cargoes. They maintained their truce throughout the winter recess, neither side firing upon the other. Colonel Herbert of the 8th Alabama even recalled that "an officer of the day on one side of the river riding along the picket lines was frequently saluted by a picket from the opposite bank, just as he would be by his own men."[14]

One day Colonel Herbert came upon a Union private with no trousers on who had actually waded the river to the Confederate side. When he drew his pistol to take him prisoner, the soldier pleaded that the Reb pickets had told him he could cross the river and would be allowed to go back after their visit.

"Colonel, shoot me if you want to, but for God's sake don't take me prisoner," the Northern soldier begged. "I have only been in this army for six months. I have never been in battle. If I am taken prisoner under these circumstances, my character at home will be ruined. It will always be said I deserted."

Touched by the plea, Herbert released the man, who splashed back into the river to return to his side. The colonel was so bothered by his act of leniency that he confessed the incident to General Wilcox, who responded, "I should have done the same thing myself."[15]

As the winter dragged on, the troops facing one another across the narrow river became, if anything, more friendly. Colonel Sanders of the 11th Alabama told his folks that one night "a Yankee band just opposite our camp struck up 'Dixie' at the conclusion our regiment cheered them struck up 'Yankee Doodle' and the Yankees cheered, they then struck up 'Home' and both our men and the Yankees cheered lustily."[16]

Wilcox and his brigade were still positioned at the ford, miles away from Chancellorsville, when the battle opened there on May 1. "Stonewall" Jackson launched his brilliant flank attack the next morning against the Army of the Potomac under Joseph Hooker after the enemy had crossed the Rappahannock upriver. From his remote, isolated section, Wilcox had no idea what was going on with the rest of the army. His orders were to

stay where he was and guard the ford until there was no possibility that the
Federals would use it as a crossing point, and then rejoin Lee.

The general, who was just getting over another attack of dysentery, frequently spent time up on his quiet picket line scanning the opposite side of
the river with his glasses, looking for signs of enemy activity now that
spring had arrived and active campaigning could be expected to resume.
This day he noticed something rather peculiar. The Union pickets had
haversacks slung over their shoulders. If they were merely on guard duty
for a few hours, they would not be carrying rations with them. Those
troops were getting ready to march! Satisfied that the ford was not threatened, Wilcox left a handful of men there and, in compliance with his
orders, prepared to rejoin Lee's army with the rest of his brigade.

When he was about to start in that direction, however, Wilcox learned
to his surprise that the Union VI Corps and part of the II had assaulted
and overrun Mayre's Heights at Fredericksburg and were marching unim-
peded up the Plank Road toward the rear of the Army of Northern Virginia. On his own initiative, disregarding his previous instructions in the
face of a dramatically altered situation, Wilcox hurried his brigade in the
direction of Fredericksburg to get in the path of the advancing Federals.
Once in position across the road, Wilcox's men slowly and stubbornly fell
back to the vicinity of a little red brick church in the woods known to the
locals as Salem Church.

As he was about to attack and brush aside Wilcox's isolated brigade,
the Union VI Corps commander, John Sedgwick, was heard to tell someone, "We're after Cadmus and we're going to pick him up." To Sedgwick,
too, it was just "Cadmus," as if everyone in the army knew whom he was
talking about.[17]

Union guns were brought up to pound Wilcox's hastily arranged line
before the infantry attacked. While the shelling was going on, a staff officer
rode up to Wilcox to tell him that three Confederate brigades were being
rushed to his support. Until they could make their way over the rough,
narrow roads in that thickly wooded country, Wilcox would have to hold
the Yankees back on his own if Lee's rear was to be protected and his victory ensured.

In his deployments, Wilcox took advantage of whatever cover he could
find. One company of the 9th Alabama was placed in the schoolhouse that
stood next to the church, and whether or not it violated any rule of warfare, another company of the regiment was crowded into the church to fire
from the windows of the main floor and the gallery. To get around inside
the building, the Rebels had to climb over the furniture that refugees from

Fredericksburg had piled in the structure for safekeeping until they could return to their homes.

Sedgwick threw shells to the right and left of the church through the woods before sending forth skirmishers to make contact with Wilcox's thin line. When the main infantry force came forward with a rush and a roar, Wilcox reported, "our men held their fire till their men came within less than 80 yards, and they delivered a close and terrible fire upon them, killing and wounding many and causing many of them to waver and give way."[18]

At one point, the Federals succeeded in surrounding the schoolhouse and taking prisoner the entire company of Alabamians positioned in it before the rest of that regiment counterattacked to retake the building and free the captured company. A second Union line came forward but was driven back into the thick underbrush. By then, reinforcements had come up and joined Wilcox in pushing back the bluecoats.

"The vigor of the enemy's attack at the church was doubtless due to the fact that they believed there was only one brigade to resist them, and that they anticipated an easy affair of it, while the number of dead and wounded left on the field attests the obstinacy of the resistance of our men," Wilcox recounted.[19]

The men in the ranks, however, had a different explanation for the ferocity of the Confederate counterattack that drove back the VI Corps veterans than that found in the official reports.

"Each Federal soldier bore on his back in this fight a well packed knapsack with several days rations in his haversack," young Colonel Sanders of the 11th Alabama explained to his parents. "These encumbrances were, as usual, immediately thrown away. . . . A Yankee knapsack is the Rebel's prize of war . . . [and] after the battle was over, I saw soldiers everywhere dressing themselves out in new underclothes of great variety."[21]

The colonel said he had heard it remarked that "Gen. Wilcox's Alabamians would not have fought so well had the Yankees not been laden with plunder," to which a member of the 10th Alabama had said, "'Yes, when we charged them, I picked out a fellow with a big knapsack on his back and I said to myself that's my man.'"[21]

So many good blankets were picked up on the field after the fighting that more than 200 could be shipped to Richmond to be stored away for the regiment's use the next winter.

As occupied as he was with his responsibilities, Wilcox demonstrated at Salem Church in just one more small way what it was that made him so well liked by the officers of both armies. In this instance, it was a captured surgeon of the 121st New York who was the beneficiary of his thoughtfulness. Dr. Daniel M. Holt wrote his wife that he had been so overwhelmed with casualties to treat that he often worked through the night. So exhausted did he eventually become that he once found himself fast asleep over a dying man.

"Had not General Wilcox kindly supplied me with food from his own table, and made me a guest rather than a prisoner, I believe I should have been compelled to throw myself down with the rest and crave the treatment I myself was yielding."[22]

Though Wilcox had saved the day with his initiative and decisiveness by preventing Sedgwick from reaching Chancellorsville, he had again sustained heavy casualties.

"This success, so brilliant for our men, was dearly earned by the sacrifice of the lives of 75 of the noble sons of Alabama and the wounding of 372 and 48 missing. An aggregate of 495," he reported.[23] Once more Wilcox had demonstrated that when he viewed it as necessary, he was ready to take heavy losses.

In his report on the battle, Lee praised Wilcox "for the gallant and successful stand at Salem Church" and said he was "entitled to especial praise for the judgment and bravery" he had displayed.[24]

The fight at Salem Church was clearly the most notable performance of the war for Cadmus Wilcox.

On May 16, when he had time to write to Mary Emily and tell her of his recent exploits, Wilcox referred once more to what was so much on his mind and, in so doing, showed that he was not motivated solely by the desire to achieve Southern independence: "If I am not promoted now, I shall be really discouraged, for I know that no one could do more than I have done with the means at my command. Everyone is talking of the injustice done me and I am now really sick with disgust."[25]

But in the reorganization of the Army of Northern Virginia into three smaller and easier to manage corps after Chancellorsville and the loss of Jackson, Wilcox found himself still in brigade command under "Dick" Anderson. Their division would become part of the newly created Third Corps, which A. P. Hill, another of his juniors, would command. Hill's successor in division command would be twenty-nine-year-old William Dorsey Pender, a former pupil of Wilcox's at the military academy. The third division, just formed and which might have gone to Wilcox, was to be headed instead by Harry Heth, a personable Virginian who was a long-time friend and classmate of Powell Hill. For whatever reason, Wilcox had been completely passed over.

To add to his embarrassment, it seemed to be generally assumed in his brigade that the general was in line for advancement. Even at his lowly level, Captain Oden noted in his diary on May 26 that he had "learned Gen. Wilcox went to Rich. today. Expect he will be promoted."[26]

For the second time, Wilcox, as a matter of pride, asked to be relieved from duty with the Army of Northern Virginia and again was not accommodated. The army was about to launch its second invasion of the North and would need all its seasoned officers. He would just have to live with his personal grievance.

As the army began its movement toward Pennsylvania in June 1863, the rest of the troops may have been in buoyant spirits, but Cadmus Wilcox was much disheartened.

Though of the same military background, there could not have been two men of more different temperament than Cadmus Wilcox and his division commander, Richard H. Anderson. Wilcox had been under Anderson since the Seven Days, and the two appeared to function well enough together. But at Gettysburg, where nothing requiring coordination between Confederate generals appeared to go smoothly, the essential difference in makeup between the two men—Wilcox always nervously active, Dick Anderson laid back to the point of indolence—became a factor at a crucial moment and helped contribute to the failure of the campaign.

And given Wilcox's frame of mind going into the movement, he was in no mood to be charitable or tolerant in evaluating the seemingly lackadaisical performance of the forty-one-year-old South Carolinian.

Longstreet knew Anderson very well from long service together and was said to be able to get a good deal out of him. But Anderson's division was no longer part of Longstreet's First Corps, and for whatever reason, Anderson, under a new corps commander, did not seem to be up for this campaign.

In Pennsylvania, Anderson, unlike all but a few of the Confederate leaders, was operating in somewhat familiar territory, for before the war he had been stationed at the cavalry school at Carlisle Barracks for several years. As a matter of fact, while in this area, Anderson had met and married a young lady who happened to be the daughter of the chief justice of the Pennsylvania Supreme Court.

Lt. Gen. Richard H.
Anderson, Wilcox's
division commander.
LIBRARY OF CONGRESS.

The drive had begun promisingly enough. As part of the Third Corps, Wilcox's brigade had marched in stages from Fredericksburg to Culpeper Court House and crossed the Blue Ridge at Chester Gap. Then the men moved up the Shenandoah Valley through Front Royal and on to Shepherdstown, where they crossed the Potomac at the same point opposite Sharpsburg where the army had crossed on its retreat from Antietam the year before. After passing through Hagerstown, Maryland, Anderson's Division moved on to Chambersburg, with General Lee and his staff accompanying the unit through the town. A few miles beyond, they encamped for three days of rest at the village of Fayetteville, Pennsylvania.

Ever since they had crossed into Pennsylvania, Colonel Herbert noted, "the attitude of the people, especially among the more intelligent, was generally that of angry defiance. In the towns and notably in Chambersburg, the people seemed by preconcert to have arrayed themselves in 'purple and fine linen' as if to let the 'rebels' see how little the war was affecting them. . . . Women looked out of their windows and sat upon door steps, dressed in silks, and often decorated with Union flags. Indeed Union flags big and little were everywhere flying."[27]

Wilcox apparently was not letting his personal frustrations affect his leadership, because at this stage one of his officers observed that despite the sourness of the reception they were getting, "the brigade as well as the rest of the army were in the best of spirits and ready and more than willing to measure results with the enemy at any time or place."[28]

Colonel Herbert recalled of his 8th Alabama, its ranks swollen with newly arrived conscripts, that "morale seemed to be perfect. We were soon in the enemy's country, and anxious for the battle that was to be final and decisive. We had no thought of anything but victory."[29]

On the morning of July 1, Anderson's division was ordered to march to Gettysburg, some fifteen miles distant. Arriving in the vicinity of General Lee's headquarters in the early afternoon, they could see that a serious engagement with the enemy was under way. The division filed off to the right of the Chambersburg turnpike and awaited orders, but the fighting ended that day without Anderson's being called upon.

At sunrise, Wilcox's brigade moved farther to the right for the purpose of taking position in line of battle. On the right of Wilcox's sector, along what the locals referred to as Seminary Ridge (for the Lutheran Theological Seminary, which sat atop it), there were some dense woods, and the 10th Alabama was ordered into the thicket to see if it was occupied. But it hardly seemed likely that the enemy had ventured so far forward of its main lines on the high ground that ran parallel and a mile apart from the position the Confederates were adopting on Seminary Ridge. To their surprise, the Alabama boys ran into a reconnaissance in force being made by the 3rd Maine and Berdan's green-clad 1st and 2nd United States Sharpshooters. The Confederate regiment had to be reinforced by the 11th Alabama, and before the woods could be cleared, a furious half-hour fight ensued, during which nearly sixty of Wilcox's men went down before the enemy's crack shots, who were equipped with Sharps breech-loading rifles.

So relieved was Wilcox at seeing the Yankees finally chased from the woods and their destructive fire halted, that he galloped up to the commander of the 10th Alabama, Col. William H. Forney, and shouted, "From my heart I thank you and to your gallant regiment I pull off my hat." With that, according to one member of the regiment, Wilcox lifted his battered straw hat with a graceful bow. "Then we had a grand yell."[30]

Now a long lull ensured for Wilcox's somewhat shaken men while Lafayette McLaws's division of the First Corps was moved into position around them and to their right, extending still further the Rebel line. When an attack plan was finally worked out by the high command, Wilcox's instructions were "to advance when the troops on [his] right should advance, and to report this to the division commander, in order that the other brigades should advance in proper time."[31]

That moment came after Barksdale's Mississippi brigade rushed screamingly across the Emmitsburg Road and by the Peach Orchard, shattering the advance Union line in front of them. The Alabama brigade started forward to continue the *en echelon* attack and, after driving some Federal skirmishers ahead of it, was able to capture near the road two pieces of a battery that the gunners couldn't get away because the horses had been killed. The gray line now dipped into a gradual descent of some 700 yards toward a rocky stream, and then began the long ascent of the slowly rising ground toward Cemetery Ridge, all the while coming under artillery fire from numerous directions. A second battery of six pieces fell into the hands of Wilcox's roaring wave.

As they got in among the guns, Colonel Herbert of the 8th Alabama observed: "One little boy in blue, apparently not more than fifteen years old, on the lead front horse of a caisson-wagon, sat erect in the midst of the storm of battle, looking ahead, spurring his own and whipping the off horse in the vain effort to escape with the wagon. The little fellow was looking ahead and did not know that the two horses behind him were shot down. I was near enough to have touched him with my sword when the dust flew from his jacket just under his shoulder blade, and he fell forward dead. In the excitement of battle, the poor fellow was killed when he was virtually a prisoner. It was horrible."[32]

Soon, however, the Alabama infantrymen became hopelessly intermingled with the men of Wright's Georgia brigade and Perry's Florida brigade, both of Anderson's division, that had advanced on Wilcox's left. There were even some of Barksdale's Mississippians in the mass crowding up the ridge. Ahead of them, they could observe fresh Union infantry coming down to shore up their broken line and defend their threatened batteries.

"Seeing this contest so unequal, I dispatched my adjutant-general to the division commander to ask that support be sent to my men, but no support came," wrote Wilcox in his official report.[33] He was too outspoken an individual, however, not to let General Lee know of his disgust with Anderson's inactivity while half of his division was so desperately engaged.

Wilcox later told the commanding general: "My Adj't Gen'l returned and reported that General Anderson said 'Tell Gen'l Wilcox to hold his own, that things will change'; that he found Gen'l A. back in the woods which were in rear of the Emmitsburg road several hundred yards in a ravine, his horse tied and all his staff lying on the ground (indifferent) as tho' nothing was going on, horses all tied."

"I am quite certain," Wilcox continued, "that Gen'l A. never saw a foot of the ground on which his three brigades fought on the 2nd of July."

On reflection, "I should have made some report or complaint against him, but I did not, lest my motives might have been misunderstood, for I had from discontent (whether justly or not it does not matter) on two different occasions asked to be relieved from duty with the Army of Northern Virginia."[34]

Motives misunderstood? Presumably what Wilcox feared was that as senior brigadier, he would be perceived as promoting himself for Anderson's command by getting him removed and creating a vacancy.

In his own defense, Anderson insisted that he was under orders from the corps commander to hold back the rest of his division and let the attack line terminate with Wright's brigade. Whatever the reason, Wilcox and the other two brigades of Anderson's division that had advanced were left in an untenable position, what with Hood's division having failed to secure Little Round Top on the right, which dominated the field. Disorganized, their officers desperately trying to restore some order, the attackers had to either withdraw from their advanced position or give up. They could not remain where they were under such devastating artillery fire and with the Union infantry constantly being reinforced.

"Without support on either my right or left, my men were withdrawn, to prevent their entire destruction or capture," Wilcox reported. "The enemy did not pursue, but my men retired under a heavy artillery fire, and returned to their original position in line."

"In the engagement of this day, I regret to report a loss of 577 killed, wounded and missing," Wilcox stated. It was the first time he had felt a need to express regret over his losses.[35]

In the morning, Wilcox's men were openly bitter about having so little to show for the heavy casualties they had taken, particularly because they were convinced that with some timely help, they could have taken the Union position. Surgeon Sanders of the 11th Alabama, no doubt hearing of what had occurred from the wounded he was treating, joined in the chorus of complaints against the division commander for his inaction and wrote his parents after the battle:

> Our brigade made a most gallant charge and broke every line of
> battle to their last one, which was composed of regulars, and had

Gen. Anderson furnished them any support (which he might well have done, as two of his Brigades had not been engaged) they could easily have routed this last line and been masters of the position.[36]

As it was, the Alabamians were back exactly where they had started the previous day and were openly questioning their leadership, the generals in whom they had formerly had such confidence.

⸻

As much of a gamble as it seemed for the Confederate army operating deep in the enemy's territory, a direct frontal assault on the Union center was being hastily organized for the third day of the battle. It would involve sending Gen. George E. Pickett's division, along with Gen. Harry Heth's and part of Dorsey Pender's, across the mile of open ground separating the opposing armies. To precede the attack, a massive artillery bombardment was planned, which Lee was convinced would soften the Federal position sufficiently for a strong, concentrated infantry assault to succeed.

Wilcox's brigade was not part of the attacking force, and his men were relieved to see that they were apparently safely positioned behind Seminary Ridge far in back of their artillery when it was observed that a heavy cannonade was going to take place.

But then they saw Wilcox walk to the crest of the ridge and survey the enemy's position with field glasses. As one of his men recalled:

> After a short while he returned and, forming the brigade in line, he moved it forward until it reached a space of about forty yards behind the artillery which was being planted near the crest. When this was done, there were ominous shakes of the head among the boys as to the wisdom of such a move, and expressions were heard to the effect that "Old Billy Fixin" (the brigadier's nickname) was not satisfied with having lost one-half his brigade the day before, but was determined to sacrifice the whole caboodle today.[37]

Wilcox was not around to overhear this grousing. After getting his men into their new position and another lengthy wait being in the offing, he rode over to the Spangler farm, where he met several other officers lolling about in an orchard near the house, including Brig. Gen. Richard Garnett, one of Pickett's brigadiers and a West Pointer Wilcox probably knew from his service in Mexico. Capt. Walter Harrison of Pickett's staff

*Maj. Gen. George E.
Pickett, West Point
classmate and
Confederate army rival.*
LIBRARY OF CONGRESS.

was also there. It was midday and Wilcox was able to produce some cold mutton for a repast. To wash it down, some "captured" Pennsylvania whiskey was being mixed with the farm's well water to make it drinkable.[38]

Garnett was not well that day and, despite the July heat, had been seen wearing his old U.S. Army blue overcoat, which he apparently removed before going into the charge. He was acutely aware that the attack they were about to make was, in his own words, "a desperate thing to attempt."[39]

When they heard the signal guns announce the commencement of the bombardment, under the direction of Wilcox's longtime friend Edward Porter Alexander, Wilcox cantered back to his command on his white pony. As soon as the Union guns began responding to the Confederates' fire, Wilcox's men started to appreciate how their commander had repositioned them. Kemper's brigade of Pickett's division had occupied the very ground behind them that they had vacated, and the Virginians were taking heavy casualties, while hardly a shell was falling on the Alabamians. But Wilcox was more concerned that none of the enemy's batteries were being disabled before the charge got underway.[40]

After the guns had been firing for an hour, and a great cloud of smoke hung over the field, the attacking infantry force filtered out of the woods and formed into seemingly endless wavy lines to begin the advance over the vast expanse of farmland in front of them. Wilcox spotted the flamboyant, long-haired Pickett and rode up to his old classmate and offered him his flask, saying:

"Take a drink with me—in an hour you'll be in hell or glory."[41]

In a few minutes, Pickett and his men all but disappeared in the dense haze, and Wilcox apprehensively awaited the outcome of the effort. In just twenty minutes or so, three of Pickett's staff officers came galloping up to Wilcox in quick succession, calling on him to advance to the support of the stalled attacking force. By the time Capt. Robert A. Bright, the third courier dispatched by the frantic Pickett, reached Wilcox, the general was beside himself.

He was standing with both hands raised waving and shouting to the rider, "I know, I know," while the courier pleaded for a chance to deliver his message.[42]

Wilcox immediately started his brigade, down to 1,200 men, forward. But where was Pickett's division? Where were the troops he was supposed to reinforce with his meager command?

As his men approached the Emmitsburg Road, they were hit on both flanks and from directly in front by Union artillery but there was no sign of any of the division they were supposed to be supporting.

Said one of Wilcox's men, "The Alabama Brigade proceeded to charge Meade's army alone. What such an absurd movement meant was never known to the officers then, nor has it ever been satisfactorily explained since."[43]

At some point, as Union infantry got into position on his flanks to rake the isolated unit, Wilcox ordered his men to hold their ground while he galloped back to seek some artillery support but could find none. After finding none of the troops that he had been ordered to support and knowing that his men could do nothing other than "make a useless sacrifice of themselves," Wilcox ordered them back.[44]

This ridiculous foray to reinforce an advancing line that had already disintegrated cost Wilcox another 204 killed, wounded, and missing and left him unnerved.

When Wilcox came upon General Lee on the field, as the survivors of the charge were making their way back to their lines in total disorder, a colonel of Her Majesty's Coldstream Guards, James Arthur Lyon Fremantle, happened to be nearby. The foreign observer said that Wilcox was almost crying as he told Lee, "General, I have tried to rally my men but as yet they will not stand."

Shaking Wilcox's hand, Lee said, "Never mind, General, the fault is all mine. All that you have to do is help me to remedy it as far as you can."[45]

Wilcox had taken heavy losses before, but it had always been in the achievement of victory, the furtherance of the cause. But at Gettysburg the losses seemed so pointless that the hardened soldier couldn't contain himself in making known those he felt were most responsible.

The summary that Surgeon Sanders of the 11th Alabama provided his family at home of the Pennsylvania experience pretty much conveyed the way the brigade looked back upon what it had been through:

> No army ever commenced a campaign under more brilliant prospects or with finer hopes for success than ours, and none I am inclined to believe ever fought more desperately to accomplish its aim. Whilst I confess that our object failed, I do not allow the impression to be made that we suffered a disaster—the whole search of the failure resolved itself into the fact that we went to Penna. and fought against a mountain composed of sand and stone which it was impossible to subdue. After two days of most desperate fighting the men came to the conclusion that an impossibility had been required of them. This position was by far the most formidable we had ever encountered, and was certainly impregnable.[46]

CHAPTER FOUR

Struggle in the Wilderness

GETTYSBURG'S TOLL INCLUDED AN EXTRAORDINARY NUMBER OF CONFEDerate generals. In the infantry alone, one of the nine division commanders was killed and two others wounded. Eleven of the thirty-seven brigade commanders had been killed, wounded, or captured. Replacing them from the shallow pool of professional soldiers on the rolls was going to be an enormous problem for Lee, and he, fully supported by President Jefferson Davis, was committed to filling the key posts in the army with academy men. At this point, only one division, that of VMI graduate Robert E. Rodes, was not headed by a West Pointer, much to the chagrin of the political generals, who looked upon these Regular army products as overrated and narrow in their thinking.

After nearly two years as a brigadier, Cadmus M. Wilcox finally got his promotion. He was chosen to replace the fallen Dorsey Pender of North Carolina as commander of the renowned Light Division, the hardfighting, hard-marching unit that A. P. Hill had led so effectively and that was arguably the best division in the army.

Advancement came at a time when Wilcox had all but despaired of ever being promoted in this army, and he couldn't conceal his surprise when Hill came to his headquarters a few days after the army had established camp at Orange Court House to alert him that he was soon to be a major general.[1] "I believe I would not be & had ceased to think about it," he wrote.[2]

Among those elated with Wilcox's advancement was young Colonel Sanders of the 11th Alabama, who wrote home:

Gen'l Wilcox has, at last, been made a Maj. Gen'l. His promotion was gratifying to the brigade, as they believed he deserved it, and it recognizes somewhat the (performance) of the brigade, though we regret to lose him as a brigade commander. The brigade has petitioned to be transferred to his Division.[2]

That appeal failed, but Wilcox was no doubt touched by a gesture made by the division commander he had so long served, Gen. Richard Anderson, who issued an order that the Alabama unit Wilcox had commanded would always be officially referred to as "Wilcox's Old Brigade," rather than by its current commander's name, as was customary.

The man who succeeded Wilcox was an extremely ambitious South Carolina lawyer named Abner Perrin, a man who was soon so disliked that a new petition of another sort was circulated in the Alabamians' camps, calling for Perrin's removal. The degree of Perrin's ambition was indicated in his writing of Pender's death after Gettysburg that "his death is a grievous misfortune to me personally; he assured me on the field that my services on that occasion should be made known and rewarded."[3]

Whatever it was that had held Wilcox back in the past obviously was no longer a factor. In recommending Wilcox's promotion, Lee wrote to Davis on August 1, 1863: "Gen. Wilcox is one of the oldest brigadiers in the service, a highly capable officer, has served from the commencement of the war and deserves promotion. Being an officer of the regular army he is properly assignable anywhere."[4]

In light of such an unreserved endorsement from the commanding general, one wonders what had delayed Wilcox's promotion until now. Was it a bias in favor of officers who were Virginians, as some from other states suspected? Or was it that he was not considered dynamic or inspirational enough for an army of rustic volunteers? In the sense that a Jeb Stuart or a John Bell Hood possessed those qualities so vital in a poorly supplied, ill-equipped force, with limited time to achieve its objectives before it be overcome on the basis of materiel alone, Wilcox could hardly measure up. If anything, he was unsettling, with his nervous disposition and absorption with detail. Even when he became casual in his attire, it diminished his appeal, his now-familiar straw hat hardly a sartorial match for Jeb's ostrich plumes or A. P. Hill's red flannel "battle shirt." Wilcox, though a seasoned professional, had been forced to wait for further advancement until combat losses had exhausted the limited group of stirring, electrifying leaders of whatever age and level of experience that Lee had available before resorting to the merely competent and dutiful.

That is not to denigrate Wilcox, who, given the fact that he had been just a captain of infantry when the war began, had done remarkably well in exercising command over large forces in fierce combat during the Seven Days, at Second Manassas, and at Salem Church. He had made an admirable adjustment to expanded responsibility and pressure. But so much more was needed of Lee's lieutenants if the army was to succeed. When Cadmus Wilcox got his promotion and became a major general, he was in simple reality the best man for the post that Lee could turn to well into the third year of the war.

When one Union officer characterized Wilcox as a "candid" individual,[5] that was probably an understatement; the man could be brutally frank in his judgments, and this lack of tact may have worked against him. This wasn't confined to his private conversations, but also was evident in his official correspondence, as could be seen again in November 1863, when he involved himself in an organizational flap concerning Brig. Gen. Jim Lane's North Carolina brigade.

Lane, Wilcox's strongest and most experienced brigadier, had gotten wind of a plot to create a new brigade for one of his colonels by having that officer's regiment removed from Lane's command and grouped with three other North Carolina regiments. In supporting Lane's protest over the plan, Wilcox wrote to the army's chief of staff:

> I have no knowledge of any effort being made to create a new brigade for some colonel who expects or hopes to be promoted, but if there should be such a scheme in contemplation, I beg that the brigade of General Lane may not be mutilated for any such purpose, and that the Thirty-third North Carolina Regiment may be permitted to stay where it is. I believe five regiments to be a better brigade organization than four.[6]

Nothing ever came of the movement, and Lane's brigade was not disturbed.

In a letter to Mary Emily on August 2, 1863, Wilcox appears to have touched on all the topics about which he felt most deeply—his deep affection for his sister-in-law, his concern for the welfare of his niece and nephew, his dread of winter, and his bitterness about the conduct of the enemy.

"If you come to Richmond you will be so near me that I can come to see you I hope," he began. "I say I hope for there are but few of us who can get leave even for a few days, now at least, but after the winter sets in regularly we can get off for a few days."

Though it was only midsummer, he already seemed to be thinking of winter as rapidly approaching, and he talked as though he fully expected that the war would continue at least until the following spring.

"It will be very trying on us if we have to winter in tents," he wrote. "I don't know how I will be able to get through the winter for I can't stand cold weather near so well as I can summer."

From commenting on the death of Sam Houston ("poor old man, his life was rather remarkable, few men will be remembered longer") Wilcox turned to the war situation to say, "I hope your coast may be spared the ravages of the Yankees."

As usual, his final words were about the children.

"Kiss the two little Wilcoxes, don't let Andy ride in the town, it is dangerous and, of course, stop Molly from using 'curse words.'"[7]

In September, the war touched Mary Emily directly when news came that her brother, John Samuel Donelson, had been killed at Chickamauga while serving on Brig. Gen. Preston Smith's staff as acting adjutant general.

She not only was depressed over her beloved Johnny's death, but she also was beginning to have deep concern over the fortunes of the Confederacy to which she was emotionally committed. Wilcox had to mask his own bitterness over the outcome of the Pennsylvania campaign to try to convince Mary Emily in an October letter not to view Gettysburg as a disaster. After citing the amount of supplies gathered and prisoners taken during the campaign, he summed up by saying, not too convincingly, "so you will see that Gettysburg was not a failure by any means."

In the same correspondence, he told his sister-in-law hopefully: "I might get a leave (as I have had none thus far) and make you a visit."[8]

In February, Wilcox obtained a twenty-five day furlough. He was becoming increasingly alarmed over the future of the South, and he had requested the leave to go to Richmond to spend time with his brother John and "have a long talk with him over the prospects of our unhappy country." Whether Wilcox had decided to engage with his brother in some political activity to influence the course of events during a period when the army was relatively inactive is not known.

When he arrived in the capital on February 6, 1864, the Confederate Congress took official notice of his visit by passing a special resolution "tendering to Maj. Gen. Cadmus M. Wilcox the privilege of a seat upon the floor of the House during his stay in the city."[9]

As a member of the first Confederate Congress, John lived the legislator's life of shuttling between the seat of government in Virginia and his home district in San Antonio, where he was active in recruiting for Hood's renowned Texas Brigade. In February 1863, he had taken a part in the recapture of Galveston, Texas, by serving as a volunteer aide (with the familiar rank of colonel) to Confederate general John Bankhead Magruder, the man Cadmus knew as "Prince John."

Recently reelected, John Wilcox had shown himself in Congress to be a staunch supporter of the Jefferson Davis administration, even advocating broader wartime powers for the president. The lively outgoing politico was, in short, very much part of the congressional scene.

The day after he reached the city, Cadmus went to the boardinghouse where John was staying and found to his astonishment that his brother, who had apparently been in perfect health, had just died of apoplexy at age forty-four.

It was Cadmus who had to break the news to Mary Emily in a letter. She did not receive word until after John had been buried in Richmond, with the Confederate Congress attending the services en masse.

Despite John Wilcox's position in public life, he was virtually a pauper. His "estate" amounted only to some law books valued at $275 and a fractional interest in some land and town lots in San Antonio. Even his burial expenses had to be paid by the Confederate government.[10]

Cadmus must have been aware of John's financial situation, for on informing Mary Emily of his death, he told her that he would send her a portion of his pay each month to help her and the children.[11]

Mary Emily apparently also knew of John's finances when he died. Many years later, a newspaper article to which she contributed pointed out that after their marriage, "his habits were such that, in a comparatively short period, his money as well as her own was gone."[12]

Ever so sensitive to the widow's plight, Cadmus wrote Mary Emily's sister Rachel, "I hope that I may be ordered to Texas so that I may be near her, what pleasure it would give me to be with her."[13]

Even though he had vowed to see Jefferson Davis himself about the matter, Wilcox was unable to obtain a transfer to the Trans-Mississippi Department to be closer to his brother's family. There was simply no place in that theater at that time for another major general.

Wilcox's other brother, young Robert, who had been on special assignment to Lee's headquarters, also died in Richmond during the war, but despite the series of personal losses, Cadmus had to try to concentrate as best he could on his vastly expanded responsibilities. He had his duty to perform.

⟶⟩❖⟨⟵

The Light Division that Cadmus Wilcox had taken over numbered about 7,200 men and in the winter of 1863–64 was the largest in the army.

Though from several states, the four brigades of the division had long been under the same commanders, men who had demonstrated their competence and in whom the troops had confidence. And not one of these brigadiers was a West Point–trained professional soldier. Edward Thomas, a planter who had had some experience in the Mexican War, headed the Georgia brigade. Alfred Scales, a lawyer, led one North Carolina brigade in the division, and Jim Lane, a thirty-year-old VMI graduate, the other Tarheel unit. A South Carolina brigade was commanded by Samuel McGowan, another lawyer with some military experience before the war.

Wilcox had had to wait long for promotion, but the command he was finally given was indeed an enviable one. The Light Division, which only Hood's could rival, had earned its reputation by its incredible march from Harpers Ferry to arrive on the field at Sharpsburg when the army was on the very verge of collapse; by its stand on the railroad embankment at Second Manassas, where, out of ammunition, the men hurled stones on their attackers; and by its performance during the Seven Days battles and numerous other engagements.

But as yet, Wilcox had had scant opportunity to test his ability to direct such a large force. Unlike the First Corps, which had been detached in September 1863 and had suffered through a costly and exhausting winter campaign in Tennessee after Chickamauga, the Second and Third Corps had been relatively inactive. Wilcox was spared the debacle at Bristoe Station, where the impetuous A. P. Hill had rushed Henry Heth's division into an attack without proper reconnaissance and had seen it slaughtered by a strong, concealed Union force. Wilcox could only regret his friend's continuing misfortune.

In November, Wilcox wrote to Brig. Gen. Ambrose "Rans" Wright, who had returned to Georgia, about another disastrous bit of troop handling that had occurred involving Jubal Early's division of the Second Corps. Almost two full brigades had been captured after crossing a bridge over the Rappahannock, when a sudden Union thrust cut the Confederate units off from the span and they were unable to retreat or be reinforced.

"That Rhappahannock [*sic*] affair tho' small was a very unlucky & ugly thing," Wilcox related. "This army has never had such a shabby accident as that before."

The letter also informed Wright that the president had visited Wilcox's camp a few days earlier, but bad weather had forced the cancellation of a scheduled review of Hill's corps, and Davis returned to Richmond. "He was looking unusually thin," wrote Wilcox.[14]

Though the winter had been uneventful for Wilcox, what Lee was able to observe of his management of his division apparently well satisfied him, because in March, when a replacement was needed for a department commander, Lee looked at his nine division commanders and advised President Davis that he had "great confidence in the ability of Generals Early, Rodes, Edward Johnson, and Wilcox."[15] The chief executive may also have noted a long feature story on Wilcox that appeared on April 23, 1864, on the front page of the *Southern Illustrated News,* published in Richmond. The article concluded:

> This gallant and intrepid officer stood high and was universally admired in the old army and if unimpeachable habits, integrity of aim and purpose, capacity and cultivation of the highest order in his profession are worth anything a brilliant destiny awaits him.

If the Confederate capital had not been aware of Cadmus Wilcox before, it certainly was now. The only fault Wilcox could possibly have found in the piece was in the accompanying sketch, which, while imposing, gave away his efforts to conceal with the comb his receding hairline.

Wilcox's first real test as a division commander came in the eerie Wilderness in May, in those tangled thickets where it was difficult to keep a company in view, let alone a regiment; where giant armies had to be maneuvered over roads that could barely accommodate a farm wagon; and where artillery and cavalry were virtually useless. But it was a theater where numbers would not count as much as positioning and alacrity of movement.

It was here that Lee believed he could minimize the numerical advantage the Army of the Potomac held over him when it crossed the Rapidan in

May 1864. The enemy army was still under George Meade, his Gettysburg foe, but with Ulysses S. Grant, the new commander in chief of the Union armies, making his headquarters with the Army of the Potomac, it was clear who was dictating the moves Lee must counter.

Ever audacious, Lee, with only two-thirds of the enemy's force, took the offensive. As soon as the Federals completed the river crossing at Germanna Ford and had disappeared in the dark Wilderness, he sent his two remaining infantry corps forward over the two roads available through the dense woodland, the Second Corps moving down the Old Turnpike and the Third Corps along the Orange Plank Road.

The Union troops, unable to see but a few yards in any direction, were startled when they were suddenly assaulted by tremendous infantry fire in their front. The advance, scarcely under way, was brought to a standstill in the thick, barely penetrable brush. Help could not be brought to the wounded hidden in the bushes. Those unable to move had more reason to panic as fires broke out here and there and began spreading, the smoke limiting visibility even further. Union officers tried somehow to establish firing lines, but their men were woefully scattered and were ready to be driven back across the Rapidan in the morning, just as they had been when they ventured into this wild region at Chancellorsville the year before.

Unfortunately, the brazen attack down the plank road had left Wilcox's and Heth's divisions in a confused, disorganized state when darkness fell over the Wilderness, the calls of birds vying with the screams of wounded soldiers pleading for help to escape the flames threatening to engulf them.

As the men fell down in exhaustion, few thought of making fires to cook rations and add to the smoke and flames consuming what little air there was to breathe in the awful region. Gray- and brown-clad figures were littered about, barely visible in the brush, second-growth timber, and tall grass. They needed rest; they had done enough that day. But their commanding officers, Heth and Wilcox, were concerned about the possibility of an attack. Their forces were in no condition to resist.

Wilcox was further unsettled by a report from an adjutant of the 18th North Carolina. The officer, William H. McLaurin, had lost his bearings and wandered into the Union II Corps lines but managed to slip away undetected and found his way to Wilcox's division. When he recognized Wilcox's white horse, McLaurin approached the general and told him that he had just left Hancock's corps and that "there was not a man between him and Hancock's skirmishers." Wilcox "evidently did not believe a word of it, and was not over polite in letting me know it," the officer said.[16]

*Maj. Gen. Henry Heth,
longtime friend of Wilcox.*
VIRGINIA HISTORICAL SOCIETY.

Undeterred, the adjutant went to his colonel and General Lane with the information, and they in turn, returned to talk to Wilcox, who by this time was already convinced something had to be done.

Though Heth and Wilcox talked with one another about the situation, neither of the two major generals and division commanders was willing to act on his own and simply arouse his troops. For some reason, both thought it was a matter for higher authority to decide. Heth went to his close friend A. P. Hill, the corps commander; Wilcox went even higher, to the commanding general.

Three times during the night, Heth appeared at the tent of Hill, who was ill and barely able to function, and asked permission to position his men, but he was told that Longstreet's First Corps was coming up and would form in Heth's front in the morning. Hill, ever solicitous of the comfort of his men, thought they were tired and needed rest and shouldn't be disturbed. When Heth continued to bother his ailing chief, Hill finally exploded: "Damn it, Heth, I don't want to hear any more about it; the men shall not be disturbed."[17]

When Wilcox talked to Lee, he was reassured that both Anderson's division and Longstreet's corps were coming up, and that Heth's and his divisions would "be relieved before day."[18]

It is not likely that either Heth or Wilcox slept that night. The one positive step they did take was to order out the Third Corps pioneers with their tools to throw up in the dark a semblance of a line. At 5 A.M., dawn, nearly four well-organized divisions of the Union II and VI Corps, which also had not slept that night, surged forward, without artillery preparation, against the slumbering Rebels of Heth's and Wilcox's divisions and sent them scampering in utter chaos to the rear. Heth and Wilcox were no doubt horrified to see their worst fears realized. Their men could put up no defense whatever. They just grabbed their muskets and fled. To help stop the rout, Lee himself rode out among the men, exhorting them to stop an face the enemy.[19]

When Lee saw Wilcox on his white pony, he told him with controlled fury: "Longstreet must be here! Go bring him here!"[20]

And like a courier, Maj. Gen. Wilcox had to gallop off down the Plank Road to hurry reinforcements up to save his own shattered command. As the men of the First Corps began arriving on the field, Lee showed his anxiety by appealing directly to the Texas Brigade to blunt the Union breakthrough.

"Texans always move them!" he called out to show the soldiers of that crack unit his confidence in them. Ultimately the breach was repaired, and a bold flanking movement by Longstreet turned the battle into a Confederate victory. But for Heth and Wilcox, it went down as a disgraceful defeat.[21]

Wilcox was too prideful an individual to even admit his division had been routed. Even after Gettysburg, where his brigade ran from the field after its isolated advance on the third day was abandoned, Wilcox insisted it had merely *retired* on his order. From the Union lines, however, the Alabamians "turned tail and fled, singly and in scattered squads, to the shelter of Seminary Ridge."[22]

In the Wilderness, Wilcox maintained that the Union success in his sector was minimal. "I was forced back about 250 or 300 yards, not a mite further," he told his friend E. Porter Alexander afterward, despite the evidence that his troops were scattered pell mell by the dawn attack.[23]

Hanging over the affair was the question of why Heth and Wilcox had not simply acted on their own in rousing and repositioning their men without involving their superiors in a matter seemingly as beneath a corps commander's responsibility as the selection of a regimental campsite.

When Heth reviewed the events with Lee—who thought enough of Harry to address him by his first name, something he rarely did when talking to his generals—Heth was told bluntly that "a division commander should always have his division ready to receive an attack."[24]

It was an admonition that applied equally to Wilcox. Both were too well schooled as military officers to have to be so reminded by the commanding general of their responsibilities.

Heth realized that Lee "knew a splendid opportunity had been lost, one that never occurred again," when the Union counterattack broke through his lines and he failed to drive the invading force back across the river, as was the commanding general's intent. As a result, the open-mannered Virginian said he was convinced that Lee "never forgave Wilcox or me for this awful blunder."[25]

And because of the episode, Lee must have begun to seriously wonder if his division commanders were not losing their decision-making ability and demonstrating a lack of self-confidence. He had to be concerned that Heth and Wilcox, too, had not been pushed, out of necessity, beyond their capacity and were feeling the pressure.

Though successfully blocked by Lee on his direct advance toward Richmond, Grant did not fall back as his predecessors had when checked. He shifted his drive farther to the left, forcing the repositioning of the Army of Northern Virginia to a point ever closer to the Confederate capital.

Now the armies confronted one another at Spotsylvania, where Lee had had time for his engineers to prepare a strong defensive line. Wilcox's sector was next to a salient in the field fortifications called the Mule Shoe, occupied by Edward Johnson's division of the Second Corps. When a great mass of bluecoats came crashing through the woods at 5 A.M. on May 12 and struck the protruding position, it quickly crumbled, and most of the Stonewall Brigade and other veteran units manning it were taken prisoner before they could stem the onslaught, including "Allegheny" Johnson himself.

It fell to part of Wilcox's division to help man an emergency line hastily set up in rear of the salient to shore up the breakthrough. Again, near calamity was turned to victory at Spotsylvania after hours of the most savage fighting of the war, battle so intense that sturdy trees in those dense woods were reduced to stumps by musketry fire.

Among the slain was Abner Perrin, in command of Wilcox's old brigade. Perrin had vowed before the battle, "I shall come out of the fight a

Ulysses S. Grant, with whom Wilcox long served. LIBRARY OF CONGRESS.

live major general or a dead brigadier." Command of the Alabama unit descended upon twenty-four-year-old John C. C. Sanders.[26]

Union casualties were fearful, but again the stubborn Grant would not give up. He continued his sidelong movement, forcing Lee to give more ground and narrow the distance to Richmond. Somehow, somewhere, the Confederate commander knew that he had to destroy Grant while there was still some room to maneuver.

"This army cannot stand a siege," Lee emphasized to his officers. "We must end this business on the battlefield, not in a fortified place."[27]

One such opportunity came on May 23, when a portion of the Union army made a crossing of the North Anna River at Jericho Mills, only twenty-three miles north of Richmond. A. P. Hill sent Wilcox's division to bag the isolated Federal units that had come over before they could be reinforced. Again, insufficient reconnaissance was done, and Wilcox was unaware as he set up his lone division to attack that he was sending it against all four divisions of the Union V Corps. The uneven confrontation that followed cost Wilcox 642 casualties and stirred the wrath of Robert E.

Lee, who faulted Hill for having launched such a piecemeal attack on the Federals.

"Why did you not do as Jackson would have done—thrown your whole force upon those people and driven them back?" he demanded to know.[28]

Again, Hill's impetuosity had cost the army, and Wilcox's command was the victim of faulty direction from a level above.

Wilcox had gone up against more than 15,000 Union troops, and after his attack had broken down, a South Carolina soldier said in disgust that whoever had planned the movement was "miserably deceived," and "it could hardly be expected that one small division, of four brigades, should rout" so many bluecoats. Among the first to break was Brig. Gen. Edward Thomas's seasoned Georgia brigade, much to Wilcox's ire. In fact, so angry was he over the failure of his attack, regardless of the strength of the Union force being confronted, that he—quite unprofessionally—publicly "cursed out Thomas and the others who failed to come up."[29]

Three weeks later near the Jerusalem Plank Road, Hill attempted to counter Grant's tactics of setting up one attacking line in rear of another but extended beyond the forward line's flank in order to envelop the Rebels' line. Hill ordered the division of Maj. Gen. William Mahone to engage Grant's forward line, and when it did, Wilcox was to be in position to take on the rear line. Mahone launched his attack and succeeded in driving the first Union line into the second to capture more than 1,700 prisoners, four light guns, and eight standards. Meanwhile, one officer said derisively, "Wilcox spent the day fumbling and fiddling about and doing nothing."[30]

Mahone, the Virginian whom Wilcox had so bitterly criticized for remaining idle and not coming to his support on the second day at Gettysburg, now had a chance to get back at Wilcox. Long after the war, he told a Union general, "This little affair . . . might have been turned into a serious disaster to the Federals had General Wilcox borne down on my firing."[31]

Of his noninvolvement, Wilcox said that Hill hadn't told him fully what he was expected to do and claimed that Mahone once more hadn't cooperated with him.

Wilcox always seemed to have an explanation, but as a division commander, he was no longer achieving the successes of Salem Church and the Seven Days, when he was just a brigadier. In fact, the highly regarded artillerist William J. Pegram went so far as to assert a week after the Jerusalem Plank Road incident that Wilcox was "fast ruining" his division.[32]

Wilcox himself acknowledged a decline in the performance of his famous unit, but without attributing it in any way to his leadership. In his August 15, 1864, letter to Mary Emily, he wrote, "I sometimes of late think they are not quite so full of ardor as they were the first two years of the war."[33]

What he might had said was that both he and his men were wearing down, spiritually and physically, as the conflict dragged on and on. The testiness among the leaders was just one more symptom of this fatigue.

"We all believe & earnestly pray that this may be the last year of the war, the Yankees I believe are tired of it too," he wrote Mary Emily that June. "It has been really a terrible war."[34]

As summer began, Lee was facing the kind of war he did not want, and one that he knew he could not win. Pressure from Butler's Army of the James on Petersburg and the vital Southside Railroad, the only means of supplying the army and Richmond by rail, had forced him to withdraw across the James and move into the thirty-five miles of prepared entrenchments extending from the capital to Petersburg in order to protect both locations. The army had been forced to surrender the initiative and was under siege.

It began in the dust and heat of summer, and even when winter's cold hardened the walls of dirt piled around them, the thinly spaced Rebels remained confined in their zigzag ditches waiting. But waiting for what? To be overrun by a Union surge they knew they were nearly powerless to resist? To fall back again? To be surrendered? What few still expected, however, was victory.

The only relief from the drudgery of the trenches came when a unit was pulled out and marched off to meet an enemy thrust at some distant point. Usually the threats were to the vital railroad from North Carolina that supplied Petersburg and Richmond. On August 25, when the Federals moved to tear up the tracks south of Reams' Station, Wilcox's and Heth's divisions were ordered out and marched some twelve miles to attack the combined force of Union cavalry and very green infantry. They succeeded in routing the bluecoats and, in addition to securing the railway, came away with 2,100 prisoners, nine cannons, and twelve flags.

The Rebels had had little to cheer about in recent months, but even this modest triumph turned sour for the proud Wilcox when he learned that a report of this engagement to Richmond said that this success was won by two brigades under Heth and Lane's brigade under General Conner. Wilcox and his division were not mentioned.

"It was my fight," he said. "I gave the orders . . . had my horse killed, one of my aides had his killed, two couriers had theirs killed & my Adjutant General wounded. My brigadiers all said it was a strange dispatch."

Wilcox and Heth were quite close friends, but when it came to military recognition, Wilcox could not allow credit he felt was due him to be conveyed to someone else. "He gave no orders," Wilcox said, "and had nothing to do with it, but to give me his brigades as I was already on the ground with mine & in the act of advancing."[35]

Given the state of the Confederacy's fortunes, it was difficult to understand the bickering over credit for this modest, isolated success without penetrating the psyche of the professional officer class, which sometimes appeared to have different interests in this war than the volunteers they directed.

Such diversions as Reams' Station were few, and the seemingly permanent quarters for the Light Division remained a jagged, four- to five-mile slash made across the clay of the Virginia countryside. As the siege wore on, morale slowly eroded, including that of Wilcox. On October 18, he wrote to Mary Emily, "This has been a most arduous and fatiguing campaign." His higher rank brought him little material comfort, he found. "Have been in a tent all the time, winter & summer."

His longing to see his family began to consume him. He felt responsible enough for the welfare and development of his niece and nephew that he had somewhere purchased a Latin grammar and an algebra book to refresh his knowledge in order to undertake their instruction personally. Proficient in languages himself, he suggested to his sister-in-law that they learn German and French. Wilcox closed by telling Mary Emily, "How my heart would leap with joy if the war would stop at once & let me hasten to your far off home to be with you and your children."[36]

Though he thought often of obtaining a transfer to the Trans-Mississippi Department to be closer to them, he did not pursue this, but doggedly went about his duties, keeping his men in the best condition possible and holding down desertions as much as he could, given the fact that so many of his troops were North Carolinians within reach of their destitute homes.

He may have been dispirited, but he was not ready to quit, as evidenced by his reaction in a letter to Mary Emily to Lincoln's reelection in November:

It may be it is better for us for with McClellan there might have been a reconstruction of the Union. But with Lincoln such a thing is not possible, and as it is independence that we are after, Lincoln is the best, for with him it is either subjugation or independence.[37]

Wilcox had occasion during that long, dreary period to communicate—albeit quite officially—with his old friend Sam Grant. Wilcox was interceding with the Union commanding general on behalf of Roger Pryor, the Virginia editor and politician who had become a brigadier general in the Confederate army and whose brigade was often under Wilcox's control early in the war. Pryor subsequently had fallen into disfavor with Lee and Longstreet and had resigned from the army in August 1863. He later returned, however, as a private and served as a special courier in the cavalry.

Pryor had been duped into being taken prisoner, and Wilcox, whether or not under any pressure to do so, was trying to secure his release. Wilcox explained the situation thus to Grant:

> [Pryor] rode up to our picket line looked for awhile at the opposite line through his glass, then dismounted from his horse, and taking from his pocket a newspaper waved it toward a group of Federal officers. One of these responded with a paper in a similar manner, and the two mutually approached for the exchange of papers. Private Pryor asked the pickets on our side not to fire. Upon meeting each other they shook hands and exchanged papers. The Federal officer than seized Pryor by the arm and led him to the rear.

As personal as Wilcox got in his lengthy letter was to point out to Grant, "I feel much interest in the case of this soldier, but cannot ask of the commander of our forces to intercede for him, for it is against his positive orders to exchange papers with the Federals, and doubtless there are like orders from yourself."[38]

Grant simply forwarded Wilcox's appeal to Meade "for such answer as you may deem proper, if it is deemed necessary to answer at all."[39] Meade did respond, telling Wilcox that he couldn't sanction "this irregular intercourse between the opposing pickets, which is in direct violation of my orders. . . . Private Pryor will have to suffer the consequences of his imprudence."[40]

Wilcox had a rather neighborly interest in the case. Pryor, when not ferrying messages for the 3rd Virginia Cavalry, had been living in Petersburg with his family until Mrs. Pryor said she "could no longer endure the strain of being perpetually under fire" in town. They had then moved to a little farm three miles outside of Petersburg, not far from Lee's headquarters. When Wilcox, whom Mrs. Pryor described as "an old friend and comrade," asked to use the green lawn in the rear of the house for his headquarters, she said, "My husband rejoiced at the presence and protection for our little family."[41]

While General Wilcox's staff officers were encamped there, the Pryors turned Cottage Farm, as it was called, into something of a social center, with A. P. Hill and his wife, Dolly Morgan Hill, Col. William Pegram, Wilcox, and others being regular visitors around the piano there. The Pryors fully expected to be situated there for "eight years, not a day less," so they had unpacked their library and hung their prized paintings.[42]

It was a rough winter physically for Wilcox, and he would have been much better off with a roof over his head than a thin canvas. In February, he wrote to Mary Emily, "I have not yet recovered my strength & had an attack of dysentery accompanied by much pain and exhaustion was confined to my bed in my tent for days, the weather was the coldest we have had during the winter."[43]

The ailing bachelor was attracting some considerate feminine attention, however. The ladies of Petersburg kept sending him nice things to eat, and he confided to Mary Emily that "when I was well enough to leave, one of them, a widow . . . sent her carriage for me & took me to her house." She could not have been nicer to him, he said, "had I been her own brother."[44]

When feeling better, the convivial—and unattached—Wilcox was probably among the Confederate generals who got together regularly in the evening at the Bollingbrook Hotel at Bollingbrook and Second Streets in Petersburg for drinks and conversation in front of a taproom fire during that seemingly endless winter. They had much weighing on their minds. A topic that may well have come up during these reflective hours was the implications of the approaching defeat of their cause for the regular U.S. Army officers who had joined in the "rebellion"—notably among them Hill, Heth, Beauregard, Pickett, and Wilcox. How they would be regarded by the authorities was an increasingly serious question for them as the South's prospects waned. There was no thought of trying to avoid or escape the consequences of their actions, however. They had taken a huge gamble in going with the Confederacy, and now they could only show their professionalism and bearing by calmly and stoically accepting their ruin.

***

The swiftness with which the end came can be appreciated by following the course of a brief, busy, and rather bizarre acquaintanceship Wilcox struck up in the closing weeks of the war.

On February 23, though still shaky from his illness, Wilcox journeyed to North Carolina with elements of his command to encourage the return of men missing from his division. In Raleigh, he was introduced by Gov.

Zebulon Vance to "a genial and warm-hearted stranger" who had just arrived in the Confederacy from England. He was the Hon. Thomas Conolly, a member of Parliament from County Donegal, who, though a sympathizer, had also rather roguishly hoped to capitalize on his long voyage through some cotton buying. Conolly succeeded only in losing his vessel to the Yankee blockade. The politician, doubtless unaware of how badly timed was his arrival, was headed for Lee's army in Virginia, and Vance appealed to Wilcox to look after the foreigner.[45]

When the visitor arrived at the Petersburg railroad station on March 15—attired in his "old leather breeches & jack boots & spurs flannel shirt & brown jacket with a haversack of provisions, pistol & Knife"—he was met by a member of Wilcox's staff and taken to the general's headquarters at Cottage Farm. Conolly's cryptic notes give an indication of how the army was getting by at this level, three weeks before Appomattox. They dined on the night of his arrival, Conolly wrote, "on Soup & extraordinary hashed beef & corn bread." During the meal, Conolly remembered, "Wilcox comes in providentially with a bottle of claret otherwise these poor fellows have nothing but water—Genl [Wilcox] has no better fare served on a plate with very seedy steel Knife & fork in his own tent."[46]

By this time, Roger Pryor's seven-month confinement at Fort Warren had ended, and upon being exchanged, he rejoined his wife at their lively little farmhouse. Conolly was invited to pay the Pryors a visit and found them "very interesting nice people." He regarded Roger as "a man of learning & intelligence." In all his socializing, Conolly perceived no hint of imminent disaster from the Southerners he encountered. It was almost as if the war was going smashingly in his restricted view.[47]

Next day, the M.P. said he went into shell-shattered Petersburg with Wilcox, who was "riding his old white charger of many battles." Again, Conolly took no notice of the siege damage. Later, Wilcox insisted that Pryor put up Conolly in his house while the general returned to his tent and continued to rough it. Everywhere he went during his stay, Conolly appeared to find plenty to drink. Harry Heth, "a most courteous, handsome man galloped up to his quarters & supplied us with excellent cocktail," he recalled. Even General Lee came up with "a flask of very old Madeira which had been in his old house & had been among the few things saved when his family had to turn out before the Yankee invaders."[48]

Always open to ways to replenish his thinning ranks, Wilcox—less than a month before the army's surrender—endorsed a proposal from officers of the 49th Georgia Regiment that they "be permitted to fill up their ranks with negroes to the maximum number under the recent law of

Congress" by instituting conscription in the regiment's home counties. In their petition, the officers pointed out:

> When in former years, for pecuniary purposes, we did not consider it disgraceful to labor with negroes in the field or at the same work bench, we certainly will not look upon it in any other light at this time, when an end so glorious as our independence is to be achieved.

Wilcox, opposed to the institution of slavery, even though he had at least one camp servant with him, scribbled on the too-little, too-late request, "Respectfully forwarded, believing that the method proposed within is the best than can be adopted."[49]

On March 27, Conolly stopped again at Wilcox's headquarters to "find him suffering from a severe boil under the arm."[50] It was disabling enough to keep Wilcox from exercising command, and management of the division fell to young General Lane, who didn't relish the responsibility. On April 1, Lane noted with relief, "Wilcox is [fit] for duty again. . . . I hope he is able to resume active command of his division and let me return to my brigade."[51]

No sooner had Wilcox resumed command than he had his horse shot twice while he was inspecting his lines near Burgess Mill. The mount Wilcox was on may well have been the much-beloved white pony that had carried him untouched through so many battles. What made the experience more chilling was that he was aware of precisely where the shots that had barely missed him came from—a Union sharpshooter hidden about 600 yards away. At about the same time and place, before his position was ascertained, the marksman brought down a Confederate artillery colonel.

As for Mr. Conolly, he could not have been more oblivious. It was a day for "tea with Genl & Mrs. Pryor & after a pleasant evening with them my comfortable room all ready as before."[52]

That next night, Wilcox recalled that his visitor "was greatly delighted when I asked him to ride with me along my skirmish line. On much of the line the Federal skirmishers were in sight."

After he had actually witnessed a clash between some North Carolina troops with a small force of the enemy, Conolly was so excited he offered his services to Wilcox for the final campaign. Wilcox told the Irishman he would make him a volunteer aide, if he wished. Conolly wanted to know whether he would be permitted to go under fire. "It would be hardly possible to escape being under fire," the general assured him.

"He said he would return to Richmond, get his baggage and report to me early Monday morning," Wilcox recalled. "Our lines were broken next morning, and the army retired toward Appomattox Court House."[53]

Conolly never got his chance to play war and must have been most surprised at how suddenly the conflict he had found so appealing came to a climax. After all, the night before, he wrote:

> Back to Pryors, Tea & game of whist which was interrupted by the most terrific bombardment of cannon & shelling lighting up the entire line of the enemy for 4 miles & thickest opp: Petersburg we sat at the window wondering & admiring the effect till 11:30 when it subsided & we went to bed not having what to think of it—Excellent sleep—thanks to the Pryors!"[54]

Wilcox, up on his line, which was stretched so thin that his men were now standing ten feet apart with no supports, observed the same bombardment with far more concern than his guest: "The enemy's batteries around Petersburg kept up an almost incessant cannonade, solid shot and shell whizzing through the air and bursting in every direction, at times equal in brilliancy to a vivid meteoric display."[55]

His friends in town had made Wilcox feel their personal protector, and he received a stream of anxious notes from them. He kept his main correspondent, a refugee lady he identified as "M.I.W.," abreast of affairs by dispatching couriers directly to her with personal messages. When word came of the disaster at Five Forks and Sheridan crushing the Confederate right flank, Wilcox alerted the woman, who was already experiencing the cannonade that would precede a general assault all along the line to exploit the breakthrough on the right.

M.I.W. recounted to Wilcox:

> The greatest excitement prevails everywhere and with everybody this morning. No one but the young people slept at all last night. The shelling was very severe from 11 P.M. till 6½ o'clock. About breakfast time they fired the warehouses and tobacco. Since then they have been shelling very horribly. The shells are whistling around us every few minutes—one has just struck nearly opposite to us. I am so sorry the enemy has gained any advantage. Every kind of rumor in circulation; people are flying in every direction; we all try and keep composed.[56]

One report had corps commander A. P. Hill seriously wounded. The lieutenant general had, in fact, been shot and killed while riding with a single courier, desperately trying to reach his command as the Union attack began. "M.I.W." closed with: "E.M., and S. unite in kindest regards for you, and say you must take good care of yourself. Please let us know if they will evacuate Petersburg tonight."[57]

When the Federals broke through Wilcox's portion of the over-stretched line, he tried to prevent them from exploiting the opening by rushing troops into two advanced forts of earth and timber that dominated the open plain in that area, Batteries Gregg and Whitworth.

Wilcox went into Fort Gregg himself, where a battery of the Washington Artillery and some 200 Mississippi infantrymen were positioning themselves for a last-ditch defense, and exhorted them: "Men, the salvation of the army is in your keep. Don't surrender the fort. If you can hold for two hours, Longstreet will be up."[58]

Waiting for the next Federal assault against the exposed position, Wilcox sat down, resting against the logworks of the fort while talking with Gen. James Lane, who felt himself in a trap at the exposed position.

"You know I didn't want to come in here," Lane told Wilcox frankly. "It was against my judgment. I don't want to be captured or killed here. You know that's what's going to happen. Let me go down there and take command, where we can dam up this gap."

Wilcox wasn't going to argue with the brigadier, one of the Light Division's stalwarts, and told him to go ahead.[59]

The Federals came in solid masses at the forts from all sides. When they got into the wide ditch surrounding the positions and made their way up to the parapets, the fighting came down to musket butts and bayonets. By the gate to Fort Gregg, the Mississippians were hurling solid shot down at the attackers with their bare hands and lighting the fuses of bombshells and throwing them when their guns could no longer be brought to bear. After one attack, when a surgeon appealed to the captain in command to surrender the place, arguing that "the army's had time enough to get in line now," the officer, Capt. W. S. Chew, replied, "Let it go as it will; we'll not give up."[60]

Wilcox, back with his infantry line a short distance away, was able to observe the inevitable overwhelming of Gregg:

> At length numbers prevailed, and the parapet of the little work
> was thickly covered with men, six flags being seen on it at the same

time; and from this dense mass a close and of necessity destructive fire was poured down upon the devoted little band within. To prevent further sacrifice and the object believed to have been accomplished, the troops in Whitworth were ordered to retire, as well as those that were near Gregg in the road.[61]

The defenders had bought enough time for Wilcox to repair his line at least sufficiently to enable an orderly withdrawal from Petersburg in accordance with Lee's design for the retreat to Appomattox. The struggle for the redoubts had been too costly for the Union forces to launch another attack in that sector.

With all he had to be concerned about, Wilcox found time to honor his commitment to "M.I.W." by sending a rider to her home to inform her that Petersburg would be evacuated that night at 8 P.M. Her response was "I am so much obliged to you for letting us hear from you. Of course we have the greatest solicitude about our friends at this critical period but trust all will be well for us."[62]

The army managed to evacuate its lines and burn the bridges of Petersburg behind it, but there was no escaping. For a week, the army dragged itself along, trying to ward off one cavalry attack after another and keep the way ahead of it open, though with no clear destination other than uniting with Joseph E. Johnston's Army of Tennessee somewhere. There was no sustenance for men or animals, and the pathetic procession slowed and thinned with every torturous mile. At one point, the caravan encountered a stream that wagons could not cross except by a single small bridge with a broken plank on it. To reach it, a flat, muddy area had to be crossed, through which ran a narrow path for wagons and caissons that could barely be made out in the darkness. In describing this bottleneck, Wilcox vividly conveyed much of what the retreat was like all along the line and what sort of leadership was required by even the high-ranking officers to keep the column moving.

> Lights were made and men stationed to warn the teamsters when and how to drive. The bridge was steep and with some of the wagons, there was much delay, balking of teams, one or two wagons were thrown from the bridge, not being able to cross, overloaded with ammunition.
>
> General Heth and myself attended personally to the crossing of the wagons at this bridge and often with our hands and shoulders assisted in getting them over.[63]

STRUGGLE IN THE WILDERNESS

But for all their efforts, stubborn leaders like Wilcox could only delay the unavoidable. With the enemy in the Confederates' front, and all their expected supplies lost, the end of the road was reached at the village of Appomattox.

While the surrender negotiations between Grant and Lee were going on in the parlor of the McLean house, a reunion of sorts was taking place outside. As officers from both sides learned what was taking place, they began to converge on the quiet, sealed-off hamlet between the picket lines and add to the cluster of blue- and gray-clad figures growing in front of the porch of the simple house across from the courthouse that had been so randomly selected for the meeting. Winks, handshakes, and whispers were exchanged as they recognized West Point and "old army" acquaintances they had not seen in years.

Union major general Joshua Chamberlain, an educator, not a professional soldier, witnessed the encounters and was surprised that "the first greetings are not all so dramatic as might be thought, for so grave an occasion.

"'Well, Billy, old boy, how goes it?' asked one loyal West Pointer of a classmate he had been fighting for four years. 'Bad, bad, Charlie, bad I tell you; but have you got any whisky?' was the response."

In faithfully recounting the sort of talk he heard, Chamberlain acknowledged that the exchanges were "not poetic, not idealistic, but historic."[64]

Union general John Gibbon, a classmate of Wilcox's who was also on faculty with him at the academy teaching artillery tactics, was in the group of idlers and observed:

> All wore an air of anxiety, though all seemed hopeful that there would be no further need of bloodshed. Here I again met Longstreet, last seen between the picket lines in front of Richmond, and Heth, an old friend and classmate with whom I had last shaken hands nearly five years before at Camp Floyd in far distant Utah. No one felt like talking much. In fact, there were but few subjects in which we felt a common interest. One question absorbed our thoughts—was the war to cease or not?
>
> To those of us, who were waiting outside, the time dragged slowly along as it generally does when the mind is on a strain for some anxiously expected event.[65]

When Wilcox arrived, he presented a rather Quixote-like figure, and Gibbon was almost taken aback by the sight of his old friend.

"There is Cadmus," somebody said, and looking up, Gibbon saw Wilcox "riding into the square on a sorry looking old grey horse, whose thin ribs bespoke the scant forage upon which he had been living."

Wilcox was dressed in a long, thick overcoat, and after he had dismounted and shaken hands all around, Gibbon asked him why he needed such a heavy coat on a spring morning.

"It's all I have," Wilcox replied, and opened the buttons to show that a shirt was all he wore underneath.

Pointing to a pair of saddlebags on his sorry horse, Wilcox said, "That's all the baggage I have left," and turning to Phil Sheridan, the Union cavalry commander who was also standing about, he remarked, "You have captured all the balance, and you can't have that until you capture me!"[66]

Union general Wesley Merritt recognized Wilcox as his instructor of infantry tactics at West Point before the war. "We renewed our acquaintance cordially but naturally he, as well as other Confederates whom I had known in days before the war were more or less constrained."[67]

What Wilcox seemed to recall most clearly of the gathering that Sunday morning at that remote courthouse village was how the Federal officers he knew "talked freely and hoped that the war was near its close, that all were tired of it."

He also remembered Gibbon's having "proposed that in the event that Gen. Lee and Grant did not come to terms and stop it that we should in the future require our men to load with blank cartridges so that no more of them might be killed."[68]

Chamberlain thought everyone there was pleased to see matters apparently coming to an end save Sheridan, who was afraid that during the truce some Rebels might seek to escape. He was for unconditional surrender.

"But the Confederate officers, one and all, Gordon, Wilcox, Heth, Rooney Lee and all the rest assure him of their good faith, and that the game is up for them," Chamberlain said.[69]

When the business inside was concluded, Sheridan, Rufus Ingalls, and Gibbon insisted that Wilcox come and see Grant again. Wilcox was still in his "winter uniform" but Grant, who had had to apologize to Lee for his own appearance that day, probably took no notice as he exchanged pleasantries with his old messmate and groomsman.

Heth, looking more handsome than ever in a new gray tunic he had put on for the occasion, also paid Grant a visit. When it came time to leave the scene, Harry found that Sam had a most welcome present for him—two gallons of good whiskey.

At some point during the day, Wilcox found himself serving as an escort for the Union artillery commander, Henry Hunt, whom he happened to meet at General Lee's tent. Hunt wanted to look up Armistead Long, who had served in Hunt's battery as a lieutenant before the war, and Lee told Hunt that Long had left his staff and was now serving with Longstreet's corps. Lee attempted to give directions to Long's camp, but Wilcox, overhearing, stepped in and offered to ride with Hunt to the place. Hunt remembered Lee on that difficult day, though "weary and careworn," was "the same self-possessed, dignified gentleman that I had always known him."[70]

When he had discharged all his responsibilities and was ready to leave Appomattox, Wilcox, a man who had claimed no home but the army since 1842, had only one destination in mind. Somehow he was going to Texas to see Mary Emily Wilcox and his niece and nephew at long last.

CHAPTER FIVE

"He Did His Whole Duty"

CADMUS WILCOX HAD WITH HIM AN UNLIKELY PAIR OF TRAVELING COM-
panions as he started off for Washington, D.C., from whence he intended
to go on to New York to book passage for a port in either Texas or
Louisiana. One was Brig. Gen. Edward Porter Alexander, the artillerist
who had directed the cannonade at Gettysburg and whom Wilcox had
known since their West Point days. The other was the eminent Elihu
Benjamin Washburne, longtime congressman and confidant of Lincoln,
and one of U.S. Grant's early boosters back in Galena, Illinois. What
Washburne happened to be doing with the Army of the Potomac at Appomattox at that time isn't clear, but he apparently was not ill at ease returning to Washington with two Confederate generals in full uniform, Wilcox
somehow having been reclad.

Provided with an escort of cavalry, the mixed party of Federals and
Confederates rode first to the train station at Burkesville, Virginia, to
board a train for the capital. Alexander recalled how, along the way, "all
Federal privates would salute our uniforms, horsemen and teamsters would
give us the roads, and in all conversations with officers or men special care
would be evident to avoid painful topics."[1]

In conversation with Washburne en route about how the Lincoln
administration would treat the conquered South, the Rebel leaders were
heartened to hear him say:

> Well, gentlemen, let me tell you something. When the news came
> that Richmond had fallen, and that Grant's army was in a position

to intercept Lee's retreat, I went up to the White House to congratulate Mr. Lincoln, and I had the opportunity to have a talk with him on this very topic. Of course, it would not be proper for me to violate Mr. Lincoln's confidence by disclosing any details of his plans for restoring the Union, but I am going to make you a prophecy.

His plan will not only astonish the South, but it will astonish Europe and foreign nations as well. And I will make you a prediction. Within a year Mr. Lincoln will be as popular with you of the South as he is now with the North.[2]

But no sooner had the group arrived in Washington than whatever warm feelings of reconciliation that were being extended toward the defeated foe were suddenly cooled by the news of the assassination of the president at Ford's Theater. If Alexander and Wilcox were recognized as Confederate generals, they stood a chance of being killed on the spot, such was the mood in the city with the assassin still being sought.

Alexander's purpose in going to the capital was an interview with the Brazilian minister for a possible position in the Brazilian Army, which was about to go to war with Paraguay. "While the streets swarmed with angry crowds ready to mob any one known to be a Confederate," the young Georgian met with the foreign diplomat and was told bluntly by the envoy that his country could not employ an ex-Confederate officer in the current climate. Alexander said he was advised to get out of Washington as soon as possible."[3]

Now wearing his old blue soldier's overcoat dyed black as a disguise, Alexander managed to get aboard a train to New York undetected and from there arranged passage on a ship to Port Royal, South Carolina.

It may well have been that Wilcox remained with Alexander during his stop in Washington and traveled with him to New York, for it was ten days after Appomattox that Wilcox finally arrived in New York—a city he knew well. By remarkable coincidence, whom should he encounter within hours of his arrival but the Hon. Thomas Conolly. Having left Richmond while the city was in flames, the Irishman, abandoning any hope of getting back to the retreating Army of Northern Virginia, made his way through the Union lines and was now about to sail home. He offered Wilcox some money and invited him to go with him to Ireland, but the former Confederate was determined to head for Texas. This time they parted company for good, and Wilcox said, "I was much pained when I heard of his death a few years since."[4]

Two months later, Wilcox surfaced in turbulent San Antonio as a civilian in the midst of the disintegration of the last Confederate army in the field, that of Gen. Edmund Kirby Smith's Trans-Mississippi Department. The atmosphere of the Texas town was both chaotic and dangerous. One man described the place at that time as full of "fugitive generals . . . and fugitive senators and fugitive governors and fugitive desperadoes as well." The outlaws were said to be "rioting in the old royal fashion, sitting in the laps of courtesans and drinking wines fresh through the blockade from France." A dozen stores had been looted and a train filled with provisions emptied and burned.[5]

The reunion of the Wilcoxes in San Antonio was brief and melancholy. Mary Emily was in desperate straits financially and burdened with two small children to care for on her own in this unsettled and unsafe environment. For some reason, Wilcox could not stay with her for long. When Kirby Smith rode into town with some of his officers in late June, bound for Mexico because the general feared arrest by Federal authorities for his part in the rebellion, Wilcox decided to accompany the man he had so long ago succeeded as brigade commander in Virginia.

Perhaps Wilcox also thought himself in danger of arrest. Maybe he saw no opportunity for himself in devastated Texas and thought he might be able to make a new life not only for himself but also for his brother's family in Mexico and was regarding his trip across the Rio Grande as a scouting expedition. Napoleon III had set up Austrian archduke Maximilian as emperor in Mexico, with the Princess Carlota of Belgium as his consort, supported by a small French army that included elements of the Foreign Legion. Perhaps there was a place in this force for an officer of Wilcox's vast experience.

It would have made Wilcox's heart ache all the more about leaving the family in such a grim situation had he seen the letter his nephew Andrew—now eleven years old and attending a German-English secondary school in San Antonio—sent to his grandfather back in Tennessee just after Wilcox departed.

"Here lately the times are so sad even the children have no more fun & enjoyment," the boy wrote Andrew Donelson, who himself had been financially ruined by the war, as he had always expected to be. "The surrender of the Southern armies have crushed all our hopes and blight all our joys and I am afraid the South will never be a happy land again. Ma does not know what to do and is waiting to hear from you before determining upon any plans for a future."[6]

Mary Emily was in dire need of employment in order to survive. When her affairs appeared most hopeless, word came that she had been accepted for the position of principal of Nashville High School. She was going back to Tennessee with her family. Whether or not her father was able to be of any help to her in securing the post, it was one for which she was eminently qualified, with her fine education and worldly exposure. It would be difficult for her to raise the children on her own while thus employed, but she would have regular income to sustain her and somehow she would manage. In Tennessee, at least she would have kin and old friends around her and would no longer be so much on her own.

Before leaving San Antonio, Wilcox had reclaimed from Mary Emily those long letters he had written her describing in detail his battles. He wanted to be able to refer to them in rewriting his reports that were lost when Union cavalrymen captured his headquarters wagons during the debacle at Sayler's Creek. While headed for a new war in Mexico, Wilcox's orderliness demanded that he have an accurate record of his involvement in the just-concluded conflict, so time would have to be made to complete that task.

And it was a fortunate thing that Wilcox did, for in the near future, when Robert E. Lee decided to write his memoirs and called on his officers to assist him by providing personal reports on various engagements—so many of the originals having been lost in the collapse of the Confederate government—Wilcox was one of the few able to accommodate his commanding general.

While a number of ex-Confederate officers then heading to Mexico were thinking of posts in the French Army, at war with the followers of the deposed Benito Juárez, others were interested in the civil posts as engineers, surveyors, and railroad administrators that the emperor was dispensing. Thousands of Southerners were crossing the border as families in wagon trains to settle the agricultural communities the ruler was establishing. This sort of colonizing was the prospect that excited Wilcox's old West Point classmate Dabney Maury, of Virginia, to go to Mexico and open negotiations with the emperor, who was enthusiastic enough about the movement he had started to learn English so that he could better communicate with the North Americans. One sticking point that Maury encountered, however, was over the status of African-Americans the Southerners had brought along and whom Maximilian insisted be treated as apprentices, not slaves.

Still another body of immigrants arriving were several hundred Rebel cavalrymen under Gen. Jo Shelby, who came armed with cannons, and fully intending to continue the Civil War from south of the border, hoping to have Maximilian as an ally. But all were headed only for disappointment.

Defying "bands of robbers and plundering deserters with which the roads were infested," Kirby Smith—mounted on a mule and dressed in shirt sleeves with a silk handkerchief tied around his neck—reached the river on June 26 and crossed at Eagle Pass. Along the way, other Rebel generals had joined the expatriates, including such luminaries as John Bankhead Magruder and Sterling Price, many of whom Wilcox knew well from as far back as their initial service in Mexico, when they were the conquerors, not fugitives seeking refuge.[7]

After spending a few days in Monterey, so familiar to Wilcox, he and Kirby Smith decided to move on by themselves. The place was filled with what Kirby Smith described as "Confederate censorians, fault finding & dissatisfied," and he was looking for a better atmosphere. Hiring a coach, the two headed for Mexico City, where they set up something of an observation post at the Hotel San Carlos, from which they could gauge what prospects there might be for the services of formally trained officers with the French military force there.[8]

Wilcox appears to have had a number of advantages to recommend him to the French authorities for a post with their army. He was fluent in French and extremely knowledgeable about Mexico, having spent so much time there during the Mexican War. Negotiations were protracted, and when Wilcox was photographed on October 8, 1865, in Mexico City with Magruder, Price, and other ex-Confederate generals, all were still civilians, looking more like a trade delegation than a group of warriors. The best offer Wilcox could procure was that of *chef de bataillon* and was holding out for a brigadier's rank. The difficulty was that Maximilian—with an American army of 50,000 veteran troops under Sheridan massing on the Rio Grande to pressure Napoleon III to withdraw his army—did not want to exacerbate the situation by putting too many former leaders of the rebellion in the United States in high positions in his army.

While he had certainly applied for a high place in Maximilian's army, it is apparent from a letter Robert E. Lee wrote him in December 1865 from Lexington, Virginia, that Wilcox was still anguishing over whether to accept a position with the French force if preferred.

A group of former Confederate generals in Mexico City in October 1865. From left, Cadmus M. Wilcox, John B. Magruder, Sterling Price, William P. Hardeman and Thomas C. Hindman. Library of Congress.

In providing Wilcox with a simple statement regarding his military career (which he had apparently requested to use in his bargaining), Lee said he was not "able to advise you on the subject on entering the military service of Mexico except as far as my judgment and feeling may be inferred from my own actions. They do not prompt me to do so; but, on the contrary, impel me to remain with my own people and share their fortunes, unless prevented by inexorable circumstances."

As for Wilcox's query regarding conditions at home, Lee said, "I must refer you to the papers for information as to the state of the country. . . . I fear the South has yet to suffer many evils and it will require time, patience and fortitude to heal her afflictions."[9]

While waiting for his demands to be met for a station he deemed appropriate to his background and experience, Wilcox found himself serving as something of a tour guide for his idle Southern associates, showing them familiar scenes around the city, such as the locale where the young American officers had formed the Aztec Club, and the Belen Gate, which he had mounted so recklessly to wave the Palmetto flag to signal the fall of Chapultepec.

As things turned out, it was fortunate for Wilcox that his bargaining with the French was unsuccessful, for, with the Civil War ended and Washington ready to belatedly invoke the Monroe Doctrine, it was clear that Maximilian's empire was to be short-lived. By the time the hapless emperor was taken prisoner by the Juárists and executed the following year, Wilcox, along with virtually all the disillusioned Southerners who had gone across the border, had returned to the States.

Upon recrossing the Rio Grande, Wilcox boldly ventured into a camp of the U.S. Army force concentrated along the river and inquired as to the whereabouts of the headquarters of Gen. George Washington Getty. Wilcox had apparently learned that Getty, whom he knew well from before the war, had confronted in the Wilderness, and visited with at Appomattox, was one of the Federal officers in the area. Of the travel-worn civilian's unscheduled arrival, an aide recalled: "I saw a pretty tough military looking man coming up the walk carrying a thin, lean, old-fashioned carpet bag."

As Wilcox approached, D. D. Wheeler, Getty's adjutant general, rose from his seat and informed his that the general was absent and asked if he could be of assistance. The unaccompanied visitor replied:

> I am General Cadmus Wilcox, late of the C.S.A., one of the last Ditchers. I'm one of those who went to Mexico, but I've had enough of it and have come back to God's country. The United States will never have a more loyal, faithful citizen than I will be in the future. I haven't anything; I want to get to New Orleans where, I think, I have some friends.

Wheeler's response to Wilcox's introduction was to exclaim:

Great Scott, is it possible! I would rather see you than anyone in the world. I was an aide-de-camp to your old friend General W. T. H. Brooks, and you whipped us so badly at Salem Heights that I would like to show you how much we think of you and how much we desire to make you comfortable. Now you be my guest until the steamer leaves Brazos next week and I'll fix you out all right.

In response to the invitation, "tears came into his eyes and he said he would accept my offer gladly; that I little knew how happy I had made him; that it was the first real soldier talk he had heard for a long time and he was happy to be back." Wheeler also observed that "General Getty, who called him Cadmus, and the other officers met him in the same spirit."

During one of his talks with his generous hosts, Wilcox showed some of his old humor by relating that at Salem Church, "when, from captured prisoners, he learned that General Brooks was in his front he determined to whip Bully Brooks (as he was known at West Point and in the regular army) if it cost him every man of his command."

After Wilcox had been idling at Getty's headquarters for a week, surrounded by veteran troops in blue against whom he had been fighting for so long, it was time to move on. Wheeler helped him by getting him transportation to New Orleans. Given Wilcox's desperate condition, all this unexpected assistance from his "old army" comrades could not have been better timed.[10]

"Without visible means of support, the question of existence became a grave problem to gentlemen whose only profession was that of arms," Darius Couch wrote of the situation men like his friend Cadmus Wilcox found themselves in after the war. "General Wilcox manfully accepted the stern logic that was thus presented to him."[11]

Upon his arrival in New Orleans sometime in 1866, Wilcox made his first attempt at a new form of livelihood in a business a number of prominent ex-Confederate leaders had turned to, trading somewhat on their names and reputations. That was selling insurance. He became the general agent for Globe Mutual Life Insurance Company of New York, with offices at 17 Carondelet, near Bourbon Street and in rear of the Customs House. For a time, Wilcox had as his business neighbor James Longstreet. In addition to becoming a cotton broker, Longstreet had accepted the presidency of the newly formed Great Southern and Western Fire, Marine and

Accident Insurance Company, with offices at 21 Carondelet, virtually next door to Wilcox. Other former Rebel officers of rank who had established themselves in the once-more bustling city were John Bell Hood, P. G. T. Beauregard, Simon Buckner, and John Magruder.

If the relations between Longstreet and Wilcox were cool, they apparently were civil, because when former Lt. Gen. Richard S. Ewell came to the city on a visit in February 1870, he told of being picked up by Wilcox to attend services at Trinity Church, where Bishop Leonidas Polk once delivered his sermons, and shared a pew with General and Mrs. Longstreet. This was rather a brave act for both Ewell and Wilcox, because Longstreet had already gone over to the Black Republicans and was advocating that the South as "a conquered people" cooperate, as a practical matter, with the party in power in enforcing stringent Reconstruction measures. Longstreet had even accepted a position from President Grant as surveyor of customs for the post of New Orleans, and as a consequence, Ewell said, "I thought I could see a good many scowling glances thrown at me in church."[12]

With Ewell being his guest, Wilcox may have been drawn into an awkward situation in joining the Longstreets. He himself had remained a staunch Democrat, like most Southerners, and no doubt agreed with his friend Daniel Harvey Hill when he said in regard to Longstreet, "Our scalawag is the local leper of the community."[13]

Wilcox showed his disdain for Longstreet's politics in a letter to Edward Porter Alexander on March 10, 1869, which he addressed "Dear Gen'l," even though he had known the man for more than a quarter century.

"He turned radical, hoping to be rewarded for it," Wilcox asserted, adding that "he always had a thirst for money." When Longstreet received letters from Northern leaders such as Benjamin Butler "congratulating him for his patriotism, boldness & rising above the narrow prejudices of his Section," Wilcox said he showed them around "with apparent pleasure, as tho it was something to his credit & to be proud of that he had recd such letters & that he was thought well of by them."[14]

Once Simon Buckner arranged a dinner party for the colony of Confederate officers in New Orleans, which was attended by Joseph E. Johnston, Wade Hampton, William Hardee, Joseph Wheeler, and others. Wilcox said, "Longstreet was invited but was not present, he told me he could not attend for it was Lent, he had then made up his mind to go to the other side & as I believe in hopes of gain." At another meeting in New Orleans in May 1869, involving a different set of ex-Confederate generals in residence there—including Braxton Bragg, Richard Taylor, Dabney Maury, J. S. Marmaduke, P. G. T. Beauregard, Harry Hays, Buckner, and

Wilcox—Longstreet was again among the missing. That was the confer-
ence arranged by Maury to establish the Southern Historical Society "for
the purpose of collating, preserving and finally publishing such material as
would vindicate the truth of Confederate history." What none of the participants realized at the time, no doubt, was that the organization they were
creating would become a forum for years of bitter literary warfare among
the South's defeated military leaders.[15]

In his flurry of correspondence with Alexander in 1869 about
Longstreet's politics, Wilcox also began to let out his harsh feelings toward
Longstreet the soldier, even insinuating cowardice on his part. In his
March 10 letter, he wrote, "I never had any respect for Longstreet's ability
for I always knew he had but a small amount. I always regarded him as
selfish & cold hearted, caring for but little save his own self."

In this letter, Wilcox made the assertion that "I can truthfully say that
I don't believe he ever saw any of his troops under musketry fire unless for
a short time & at long range at 2nd Bull Run & Gettysburg."[16]

Earlier, on February 6, Wilcox had apparently filled out a question-
naire Alexander was circulating for a history of the First Corps he was
undertaking at Longstreet's request. Wilcox, addressing his response "My
Dear Sir," said he had completed the form "as well as I can at this time," as
he was "suffering with cold in the head, sore throat & pain in chest."

But in his cover letter, Wilcox had been even more explicit about
Longstreet's conduct in battle, expressing a view that went in the face of a
mountain of evidence to the contrary and left him almost alone in his
denunciations of the corps commander he so bitterly disliked. Even
Lafayette McLaws, a First Corps division commander, expressed views sim-
ilar to Wilcox's regarding Longstreet's personality and character, but he would
never suggest the man ever showed fear or even nervousness under fire.

"He is spoken of as the hard & stubborn fighter, his troops did fight
well, but not from any inspiration drawn from him," Wilcox maintained.
He said further:

> The Second Bull Run was the first place that I ever saw
> Longstreet where he could see his people in the fight & he was then
> only under artillery fire where he went after that I don't know. At
> Gettysburg I saw him under artillery fire the 2nd day & these were
> the only places that I ever saw him in battle.

After having vented all this to Alexander—though the veteran artillerist
had probably been just as good a witness to the corps commander's personal
conduct during the war—Wilcox added something rather remarkable:

As he has requested you to write the history of his corps . . . I suppose you are good friends, & so am I his good friend & these points are mentioned to show how history is or may be made. You can burn this letter when you read it if you choose.[17]

All these things were being said before Longstreet became an object of deep scorn in the South for his politics, before he had become head of the metropolitan police and the black militia in New Orleans and led them in a bloody clash with a mob of former Confederate soldiers in 1874.

⟶⟶⟶⟵⟵⟵

While Wilcox was weathering the turmoil of Reconstruction in New Orleans, a time when the beauty and charm of the city seemed visible only to the artistic eye of the visiting Edgar Degas, another dramatic change came about in the life of Mary Emily Wilcox. In 1874, the widow, who was now teaching music and languages at Adams Seminary in Nashville, was offered a position as a translator in the Post Office Department by President Ulysses S. Grant, a man she then and subsequently regarded as "my true and unchanging friend," though one wonders how they ever became acquainted. If old friends in Washington had played a hand in bringing about her employment (and even if the president himself had not taken a personal interest in the hiring of a government clerk), Mrs. Wilcox was more than qualified for the position proffered, being fluent in six languages.

She was delighted to have not only a government position to depend on for her financial security, but also the opportunity to return to the nation's capital, where she had been born under such unique circumstances and in whose cultivated society she was so comfortable.

Accompanying her north were her son, Andrew, now twenty, and her blossoming, seventeen-year-old daughter, Mary Rachel. Soon after her arrival, Mary Rachel was referred to by a social scribe as "one of the most attractive and accomplished young ladies in Washington."[18] Though Mrs. Wilcox's salary was modest, she was able to enroll her daughter in the Academy of the Visitation in Georgetown, where Mary Rachel exhibited distinct literary talent and had several poems and essays published in various periodicals.

Andrew Wilcox, who had been carrying on the family's military tradition by attending the Virginia Military Institute, also went to work for the Federal government. He obtained a clerkship in the Navy Department, which he retained for some years.

Whether prompted by a desire to be closer to his relatives or strictly by business considerations, the same year that Mary Emily relocated in Washington, Cadmus Wilcox also made a major move. He became the manager of the Maryland department of the Life Association of America with offices in Baltimore, just 40 miles from Washington, and took up residence at the St. Clair Hotel. He remained a guest there for more than two years, living what must have been a rather lonely bachelor's life.

Four years after he arrived in Baltimore, the city directory carried a listing for "C. Marcellus Wilcox" at 163 St. Paul Street, suggesting Cadmus had finally moved from the hotel to a rooming house but did not wish to be readily identified at that location by his familiar first name.

Curiously, it was not until after the Grant administration ended that Wilcox moved to Washington. Though a place had been found for his sister-in-law on the government payroll, Wilcox—who had, after all, been Grant's groomsman and had known him for decades—did not become part of his administration in any capacity. The explanation was no doubt political. Given his attitude toward Longstreet's having turned Republican, he probably couldn't bring himself to accept a position from Grant even if offered, an unlikely gesture given Wilcox's outspoken Democratic leanings.

In 1879, however, Wilcox gave up the insurance business and went to Washington without a job. Before long, according to Darius Couch, "old army" friends in the city "were enabled to secure for him honorable employment in the public offices."[19]

Honorable employment? The truth was that Wilcox, now fifty-five, was hired as a messenger in the U.S. Senate at a salary of $1,800 a year.[20] His fortunes had sunk to the point where he was forced to become a courier in the halls of government serving Congressmen whom in the war he had either commanded or fought against as enemies.

Later Wilcox was elevated to the position of "acting assistant doorkeeper" of the Senate, a post in which he supervised the pages and monitored access and communication to the floor as he once had directed regiments and brigades.[21]

An unexpected development that brought some joy to Wilcox's life in April 1879, and no doubt bolstered his self-esteem, was the receipt of a letter from a former Union officer who was now practicing law in Baltimore, Harrison Adreon.

The attorney said he had been trying to locate Wilcox for some time to return something that had been in his possession since the closing days of the war. That was Gen. Robert E. Lee's letter to Wilcox of November

12, 1862, in which Lee had stated that he could not possibly spare him from the Army of Northern Virginia. Adreon explained:

> The letter in my possession addressed to you by General Lee was picked up by me from among scattered papers lying in the road just where Sheridan had captured & destroyed a portion of the Confederate wagon train.
>
> I concluded it was a letter that would be prized by the gallant soldier to whom it was addressed—one who from personal experience I had always found in front of our troops whenever a battle was raging—and as it contained such a high compliment to you as a soldier from your old chieftain, Gen. R. E. Lee.[22]

Wilcox apparently lived in the same house as Mary Emily and her children at some times and apart at others, but they always remained in close contact. In 1889, for example, he wrote a letter from 1213 H Street in which he told a friend by way of one of his frequent medical reports that he "had quite a knockdown in the shape of a regular old fashion ague (not chill)" and "had difficulty in getting back to [his] quarters." The old soldier may have instinctively still referred to wherever he was living as his "quarters" but it would seem odd that he would refer to his home with the other Wilcoxes that way.[23]

But even when not domiciled in the same house, it is clear that Wilcox closely looked after his relatives and was reluctant to be far from them. Classmate Couch, who was in the city during that period, wrote that "it was the fixed purpose of his life not to be separated from these relatives for whom he felt the most tender solicitude, and over whom he extended the gentlest care." Whatever he must endure from his superiors in this Yankee government to earn his living, Wilcox at least "found in this cultivated family circle the charms of a refined and loving home."[24]

One can only imagine what the quiet evenings in the parlor must have been like with Mary Emily, who read her favorite French authors—Hugo, Moliere, Zola, and Daudet—in their own language, and Cadmus, knowledgeable enough to have translated military works composed in French, in conversation. Or the sounds that must have emanated from her little house at Dupont Circle as she played the works of her cherished Beethoven and Mendelssohn at the piano.

Though it was a modest dwelling, Mary Emily always had on display there the numerous artifacts she had inherited that dated from her family's service to President Jackson, including "Old Hickory's" walking cane, his saber, and his pistols. In her possession also was a large, velvet bound book containing correspondence between Jackson, Tyler, Madison, Monroe, Van Buren, Polk, and other historic figures.

Once when she entertained, a social note in a newspaper pointed out that "the hostess and her pretty daughter were assisted in receiving by General Cadmus Wilcox."[25]

One opportunity for military service abroad came for Wilcox during this time from the khedive of Egypt, but unlike his friend Charles Field, a former major general in the Army of Northern Virginia who had lost a leg in the war, Wilcox declined the offer to don a fez and go off to the Middle East to practice his profession. He preferred the Washington scene.

After the misery of the Reconstruction years had passed and the one-time Confederate generals had situated themselves in some other endeavor, they found the time to begin squabbling among themselves and pointing fingers at which were responsible for the South's military defeats and lost opportunities. Wilcox was not hesitant about becoming involved, going to war with a pen against men he had known for decades.

It was the sort of conflict that did little to enhance the reputations of any of those who chose to participate. Wilcox's name usually appeared in the *Southern Historical Society Papers,* a popular monthly forum for this literary combat, but some of his most vicious comments were in private correspondence with fellow officers throughout the South. He had been brutal in his criticism of Lt. Gen. Richard H. Anderson at Gettysburg in his communications with Lee when the commanding general was compiling his memoirs at Washington College. It was with Longstreet, however, that Wilcox became most bitterly embroiled. Responding to the First Corps commander's criticism of his handling of his brigade at Gettysburg, Wilcox counterattacked furiously in the pages of the *Southern Historical Society Papers* in 1878:

> General Longstreet's two contributions to the Philadelphia Weekly Times have been shown to abound in misstatements, gross exaggerations and to savor somewhat of self-laudation; his exposition of the battle of Gettysburg is not such as a professional soldier of his long service and high rank should have given to the public, to say nothing of the manner of its preparation.

There is much exaggerations and high coloring in his description of the engagement during the afternoon of the 2nd. This comes from the fact of its having been written by a sprightly young newspaper man, Henry W. Grady.

The official reports, Wilcox maintained, "made clear that General Longstreet did not attack as he was ordered, to say nothing of his long delay, which has not as yet been satisfactorily explained."[26]

In a personal letter to Daniel Harvey Hill long after the war, Wilcox showed that his bitterness toward the corps commander he had known for so many years had not subsided: "I have always to restrain myself when I think of him, as a soldier, for I had a poor opinion of his ability and had . . . a suspicion he was selfish, and indifferent to others."[27]

Longstreet, on his part, took every chance to put down Wilcox. In his memoirs, he got in a dig about Wilcox's behavior at Seven Pines—a battle fought nearly a quarter century earlier—contrasting him with one of his lasting favorites, George E. Pickett.

"General Wilcox received the order to retire, and in undue haste pulled his command out, assumed authority over Pryor and ordered him off. Pickett, the true soldier, knowing that the order was not intended for such emergency, stood and resisted the attack." All Wilcox had done in carrying out what the corps commander considered a "precipitate retreat" was to promptly obey Longstreet's command.[28]

The *Philadelphia Weekly Times* pieces to which Wilcox referred appeared in 1877. In his November 23 article, Longstreet had cut Wilcox deeply by asserting:

> General Wilcox steps forward as a willing witness in all concerning the battle of Gettysburg, and seems to know everything of General Lee's wishes and the movements of the First Corps and in fact everything else but his own orders. His brigade was the directing brigade for the *echelon* movement that was to protect McLaws' flank. He went astray at the opening of the fight, either through ignorance of his orders or a misapprehension or violation of them. Had he but attended to his own brigade instead of looking to the management of the general battle, the splendid exhibition of soldiery given by his men would have given better results.

In response, Wilcox abandoned any pretense of merely professional differences with Longstreet and admitted to the personal animosity that existed between them:

I am quite certain the readers of the Weekly Times do not care to know of the indifferent opinions General Longstreet and myself entertain for each other but as he has made public his estimate of me I may in turn say that I never regarded him either as an efficient or able officer, though greatly distinguished in our late war, and having the good fortune to command a superb body of men.

While being credited for his gallantry at Williamsburg, Longstreet kept himself so remote from the fighting that "of his own personal knowledge, he knows but little more than the man on the moon," Wilcox asserted.[29]

The long-maintained feud between the two may well have contributed to the difficult time Wilcox had in gaining meaningful government employment in Washington, because Longstreet was much in favor with Grant's and other Republican administrations. Like most Southerners, Wilcox remained a die-hard Democrat. As a matter of fact, when Gen. Winfield Scott Hancock was defeated in his run for the presidency in 1880 as a Democrat, Wilcox was one of the first to visit Hancock at his army headquarters on Governor's Island in New York City to extend his regrets.

In that, Wilcox, who so many years before had been stationed there, followed on the heels of an old classmate also on the outs in Washington, George B. McClellan, who had had the temerity to run against Abraham Lincoln in 1864 for the presidency. Wilcox had maintained close contact with McClellan since the war and, in fact, had visited him in 1879 when he was governor of New Jersey, marveling at his ability to administer the state's affairs while visiting the state capital only one day a week. Later, Wilcox was the house guest of McClellan's in-laws, the Marcys, at Orange, New Jersey.[30]

As late as 1886, Wilcox showed his political sentiments when he wrote a friend that "the South can be nothing but democratic, there is nothing else for it to do but to oppose the republicans, for they have reason to hate and distrust it."[31]

Wilcox's writings on the Civil War were not extensive—several articles and some carefully organized official reports of engagements. He roughed out a few pages of a memoir. His main literary interest, it seemed, was in preparing a detailed history of the long-ago Mexican War, a treatment so extensive that it occupied him for decades. It was a project that few were in better position to undertake and was so definitive that it included rosters of officers and units that participated in the conflict.

When he had to refer in it to the further careers of participants, Wilcox, curiously, could not bring himself to use the term Civil War, preferring to say simply "the late war." He worked on the manuscript for so long that it seemed as if it would never be completed, so careful was he in his accurate depictions of events. In fact, so concerned was he about accuracy that after the editor of the *Southern Historical Society Papers* inserted a couple of seemingly minor errors in the editing and printing of one of his articles, Wilcox demanded that in the future, "nothing that I should send you ought to be published until sent to me for correction."[32]

Remarkably, the Aztec Club, which Wilcox had helped found in 1847, had managed to endure over the years. After the interruption of the Civil War, meetings resumed in 1867, and thereafter the group got together at least annually. The sessions provided an opportunity for former Union and Confederate officers to relive their common experiences as much younger men at Chapultepec, Churubusco, and other ancient battles. On September 14, 1881, the organization got together at Wayne, Pennsylvania, outside Philadelphia, with twenty-two members present. The procession of middle-age men filing into the banquet hall, all but a few in civilian attire, created an extraordinary—and to the outsider, a seemingly incongruous—assemblage of national figures.

Coming from Washington, New York, and other parts of the country were former president U. S. Grant, back from his triumphal world tour and not yet having suffered the financial losses that would devastate him; William Tecumsah Sherman, now commander in chief of the U.S. Army; Joseph E. Johnston, just having completed a term in the House of Representatives; Fitz John Porter, still awaiting vindication after having been cashiered from the army for "disobedience, disloyalty and misconduct in the face of the enemy" at Second Bull Run; and Cadmus Wilcox, the acting assistant doorkeeper of the U.S. Senate.

Part of the business at this particular session, which featured a railroad outing during the day and included as the society's guests many leading newspaper editors and publishers as well as elected officials, was the induction, belatedly, of a new member who had earned brevets at Contreras and Molino del Rey back in 1847 with the 8th Infantry. For some reason, he had never joined the club. He was the newly appointed U.S. marshal in Georgia, James Longstreet.

Wilcox was an active member of the select group, involving himself in such touchy matters as the election for the presidency in 1881.

"I fear some may want Grant, others [Winfield Scott] Hancock," he wrote to a club official on September 2. "These two members are not on the friendliest terms & should they be brought into collision on even as inconsequential as affair as the presidency of our club, it might be the cause of bad feeling extending to other parties." He personally favored Gen. William Preston of Kentucky as a safer choice, but in a way, Wilcox's sensitive, behind-the-scenes maneuvering to avoid a clash between two men of whom he was fond demonstrated just one more reason why he remained so popular among so many of his associates.[33]

With the inauguration of Grover Cleveland in 1884, the first Democratic administration since the end of the war, the plight of a number of ex-Confederates in Washington markedly improved, Wilcox among them. Harry Heth, who had been employed by the government as an engineer, became inspector of Indian agencies. Joseph E. Johnston, perhaps Wilcox's closest friend in Washington, though many years older, was named U.S. commissioner of railroads. At first the new president, who himself had hired a substitute and did not serve in the army during the Civil War, tried to arrange a position in the Korean military for Wilcox. Wilcox's friend Gen. Philip Sheridan encouraged him to accept the appointment, but he still declined to leave Washington. The job Cleveland found for him instead was chief of the railroad division of the General Land Office, and he held this position until the end of the administration, though the main responsibility for overseeing the railroad industry was transferred during this period to the newly created Interstate Commerce Commission.

Cleveland also came to the aid of Mary Emily Wilcox, who had encountered a serious problem with the previous administration, that of Chester Arthur, and had appealed to the incoming president to remedy her situation.

Mrs. Wilcox had held her clerkship in the Post Office Department for eight years and received four promotions, when she saw in the newspaper that the Republican members of Congress were demanding her dismissal because, as the widow understood the motivation, "having been born in the White House, I had no claims on Tennessee and was moreover, a rebel and a democrat." She continued:

> I hoped the report was not true, for no family was so identified with the history of Tennessee as the Donelson. . . .
> I had always avoided politics in office and often when stung to the quick by the cruel attacks of my office associates on the Southern people had kept silent.

She traced her trouble to her consistent refusal to contribute financially to the Republican party when called upon over the years.

After the newspaper report appeared, Mrs. Wilcox paid a visit to Postmaster General Timothy O. Howe to inquire if any charges were being made against her. She said she was told bluntly by Howe: "Yes, madam, serious charges. They tell me you are a rebel, that you have been heard to speak of Jeff Davis as President Davis, that you refused to contribute to the campaign fund."

When she asked about whether her work had been satisfactory, Howe allegedly responded: "Yes, madam, they say you are a very smart woman, smart enough to get along without government help."

Though not dismissed, she was moved into a lesser, lower-paying post that she described as "a miserable little place, under everybody, but necessity forced me to accept it."

The tasks heaped upon her ranged from translating some essays from Italian health boards on cholera to translating from the German the bookkeeping methods of the German Imperial Post Department.

Her plight elicited sympathy in official circles. Eight senators went to see President Arthur about the way the widow was being treated. Even seventy-year-old Alexander Stephens left his sickbed to pay her a visit. Too ill to leave his carriage, the former vice president of the Confederacy and currently a member of the House of Representatives called Mrs. Wilcox from her house to tell her "not to be downcast at this rascally business" and blamed her trouble on old political enemies of Andrew Jackson, with whom the Donelsons were so closely associated.

Mrs. Wilcox laid all this out in a long, audacious appeal to President Cleveland for a better position in government, assuring him, "My father and husband were Union men and until after the fall of Fort Sumter opposed secession" and that "I desire above all things the success of your administration . . . and the perpetuity of Democratic control."[34]

Her plea was accepted by the president, and she was soon given a more satisfactory position in the Treasury Department. For decades she was a familiar figure at the opera and concerts in the city, as well as at the openings of virtually every art exhibition, a stocky, auburn-haired figure whose "taste in dress has been settled for her by the almost constant mourning which she has worn since her girlhood."[35]

Since taking up residence in Washington, Wilcox tended to socialize primarily with active and former U.S. Army officers he had known from before the war, and the colony of Southerners who had moved to the capital as either elected officials or government employees. It would appear likely that his circle included the lively widow of one of his closest associates who was also reliant for a time on menial government positions for her livelihood, though eventually her writing and public appearances became her main income source. That was the wife of the late George E. Pickett, LaSalle Corbell Pickett, who resided at the Ontario Apartments with Mary Elizabeth Torrance for many years.

In 1886, perhaps drawing on his long-ago association with Alabama troops during the Civil War, Wilcox applied for the presidency of the University of Alabama when it became vacant, but the position went to someone else. He attributed his being passed over to politics, saying to a friend, "it looks as though the position might degenerate into one to be bought & filled by politicians, this would be a misfortune."

Still, he insisted that he was not too distressed at the result:

> I had not set my heart upon that Presidency, yet I would have taken it and set about to make it, and myself, too, a success.
> There are not many men who have been in the world as long as I have who would prefer Tuscaloosa to Washington, nor do I.[36]

Four years later, however, when the post was again open and former Gov. Edward O'Neal urged him to seek it, Wilcox decided to launch an all-out assault to capture it. His government paychecks apparently had come to an end with the Cleveland administration, and though now sixty-five years old, he was in need of new employment. But the almost desperate old soldier's effort turned out to be a deeply humiliating experience.

O'Neal, a one-time colonel in the Army of Northern Virginia who, like Wilcox, had commanded an Alabama brigade at Gettysburg, had strongly advised him to make a special journey to Tuscaloosa to present himself in person to the university board of trustees when it met to consider filling the vacancy. Wilcox went fully armed with letters of endorsement he had hastily secured from "Joe" Johnston, Rep. Joseph Wheeler, Rep. William H. Forney, and other prominent Confederates with whom he associated in the district.

Wilcox left Washington on a Saturday morning in June and, encountering several delays, did not arrive in Tuscaloosa until Monday morning.

Wilcox conveyed the details of his rather pathetic mission in a letter to a friend:

> The heat was intense. I reached Tuscaloosa to find myself with an attack not exactly of Cholera Morbus but the next thing to it, which weakened me & took away my appetite.

After an effort to sleep and the lightest of breakfast and a "whiskey toddy" which did me good, I rode out through dust and sunshine to the University Building.

The board was in session, and Wilcox was kept waiting. He was much relieved when a friend on the staff, seeing his shaky condition, "bade me make the Library my headquarters."

After a while, still feeling unwell, he went back to his hotel to lie down without ever having been called before the trustees. But he returned late in the afternoon when the commandant invited him to judge a drill contest between the four companies of cadets at the quasi-military institution. The local newspaper reported the next day, to the former Confederate major general's chagrin, that "Col. Wilcox of the U. S. Army was one of the judges at the drill the afternoon preceding."

While kept cooling his heels for an interview before the full board, Wilcox encountered several trustees who expressed support for his candidacy and even met the governor, who served as board president, and his wife, "and made apparently a good impression on both."

As it turned out, when Wilcox was called, it was to let him know that a choice had been made before he even had a chance to present himself for an interview. Again, Wilcox suspected that politics had been involved. He told his friend of a commitment the governor supposedly had to the person selected for previous support in his bid for a Senate seat, and how another trustee wanted to back Wilcox but was in a fix because his brother was an applicant for a contract for penitentiary convicts and didn't want to jeopardize it by going against the governor.

Probably the most uncomfortable part of the affair was that after being told the presidency was going to someone else, Wilcox was invited to dinner by the board of trustees, and he gentlemanly accepted before journeying back to Washington in solitary defeat.[37]

On a gray November morning that same year, 1890, Wilcox was walking on G Street, across the mall from the White House and at the base of Capitol Hill, when he tumbled into an excavation that a railroad construction crew had left unguarded. The old soldier who had gone through the thick of the Mexican War, various Indian wars, and the Civil War unscathed struck his cheek hard. According to a newspaper account, a passerby saw him fall and helped him, bleeding profusely, to his room. His family was summoned, and for five days he lapsed in and out of consciousness before succumbing to what doctors determined was a brain hemorrhage.

So familiar a figure was he in the city that a headline in the *Washington Post* announced simply "GENERAL WILCOX DEAD." It was not until a foot down in the column that any reader who did not know him learned that his rank had been attained in the Confederate States army, not the U.S. Army.[38]

A simple funeral was held from St. Matthew's Church in Washington. It was attended largely by army officers Wilcox had known. Three Federal generals—Parks, McFeely, and Casey—were honorary pallbearers, along with three Confederate generals—Heth, Charles Field, and Beverly Robertson. Sen. Zebulon Vance of North Carolina came, as well as Congressmen Wheeler and Forney. Accompanying Mary Emily to the service from her home at 2021 O Street, where earlier in the year Wilcox also had been residing, was Joseph E. Johnston as chief mourner. Now eighty-three years old, Johnston had been more closely associated with Wilcox in recent years, through their involvement in railroad supervision, than he had been since the war.[39]

Following his death, Wilcox's niece, Mary Rachel, used her literary talent to set about editing his manuscript on the Mexican War and arranged for its publication in 1892. The work received extremely favorable reviews from major newspapers around the country, but the reaction that Wilcox might have cherished most was that of the Aztec Club, which at its annual meeting in New York declared that the book would go down as "the most reliable and interesting history of the war ever written, and as such the club strongly recommended it to the Government and the people generally."[40]

That his *History of the Mexican War* was not brought out while the author was still alive to appreciate its reception provided just one more tragic touch to Wilcox's later years. His role in that conflict would also be remembered by the conspicuous position given young Lieutenant Wilcox in the massive painting *Storming of Chapultepec,* hanging in the Capitol, the place where he served in such modest fashion.

A lengthy obituary in the *New York Times* noted:

> The career of Gen. Wilcox had its turning point when he chose to espouse the cause of the South at the outbreak of the rebellion. Before that time he was an army officer with a record for brilliancy and in the enjoyment of prospects well calculated to satisfy a soldier's ambition. He rose to the rank of Major General in the Confederate Army, but it brought him no permanent advantage or honor, and in

his declining years he was glad to accept a place as messenger in the Senate.[41]

But the writer was wrong about lasting esteem. Although the war and his decision to go with the Confederacy had indeed cost Wilcox dearly, he never lost the regard of most of those with whom he had served. After his passing, the sensitive Harry Heth said of Wilcox:

> I know of no man of rank who participated in our unfortunate struggle on the Southern side who had more warm and sincere friends, North and South, than Cadmus M. Wilcox, and over whose sad demise more sincere tears were shed.

In summing up the career of the man he had known for so many years, he wrote, "Energetic, brave and conscientious, he did his whole duty."[42]

Cadmus M. Wilcox conveyed his basic attitude toward life in a single sentence when he once told Mary Emily, "We must live out our troubles successfully and with a manner in the world that we may be proud of."[43]

No matter what humiliation was imposed upon him as a result of his having taken the course he did in the Civil War, he never showed his hurt nor gave his enemies the satisfaction of seeing him cowed.

Whether it was to call on a prospect for an insurance policy or deliver a message to the Senate floor, he maintained his bearing as a professional army officer and, in fulfilling his responsibilities with his air of formality, elevated the dignity of the positions he was compelled by circumstances to occupy.

To him, the only degradation to be avoided was becoming too vain a man to do what he must to subsist on his own. In this, his attitude was akin to that of another Confederate general, one he had not particularly admired during the war, Lt. Gen. Richard H. Anderson of South Carolina. When Anderson's financial situation became desperate after the war, he did not hesitate to join a railroad gang and pick up a tool as a day laborer to support his family. Ultimately, it was the president of the line, not the general, who was embarrassed by Anderson's situation, and he found a clerical position for him in his Camden freight office.

Despite his reduced station in life, Wilcox continued to mingle comfortably after the war with generals, diplomats, and Congressmen, not with shame but as someone who had all the requisite credentials for acceptance. He was a man who by intellect, education, and experience could as well join in a discussion of Napoleonic strategy as blend into the audience in the lobby of a concert hall.

What he did tenaciously protect was his military reputation. He could suffer putdowns in the world of commerce without a whimper, but any suggestion that he had somehow failed in the performance of his duty on the battlefield was met with the most vehement response, even if it meant having to sometimes exaggerate the truth of the matter, such as when he defended the performance of his command at Gettysburg and in the Wilderness.

He had worked too hard to achieve his military status, and though he may have been willing to accept a lowly status in the civilian world, he would never accept a military post he thought beneath his qualifications, as evidenced during his negotiations with Maximilian in Mexico.

His achievements during the Civil War were not of the sort to attract the attention of the public and the press as did colorful characters such as Beauregard and Jeb Stuart. It was the more famous generals he served who could most appreciate the difficulties and importance of his work at Frayser's Farm, Second Manassas, and Salem Church.

That is not to say that Wilcox did not covet military recognition. Indeed, he hungered for it, for he was in a profession where every man's prowess was constantly being measured against that of his contemporaries, the pace always being carefully charted on the calendar. But he must have recognized early on that he was not going to emerge as one of the great captains of the war.

Although Wilcox at times seemed livid with rage over the depredations of the Yankee soldiers upon Southern civilians, he never seemed to have any criticism of the officers who commanded them and, indeed, was able to socialize congenially with Sherman and Sheridan after the war when most Southerners had nothing but loathing for them for the destruction they had wrought.

When the war was finally over, Wilcox seemed almost anxious to put it aside as something that had been imposed upon the West Point officers, an affair not of their making. He much preferred to reflect on the Mexican War, when they were all young and enthusiastic participants fighting side by side.

His relationship with Mary Emily Wilcox, who continued to reside in Washington until her death on August 28, 1905, seems to have been one of assuming responsibility for the welfare of a dear brother's widow and offspring. Andrew Wilcox showed his affection for his uncle by naming his firstborn child Cadmus Marcellus Wilcox.

But as it became apparent that Wilcox was able to do little for his relatives financially, and their survival was attributable more to Mrs. Wilcox's high intelligence and tireless determination than to his material aid, a different relationship came to exist between them. It became clearer that it was Wilcox—the bachelor soldier—who was deriving from this fragment of a family what was missing from his own life. It was Mary Emily and her bright, gifted children who nurtured him at a time in his life when he was most in need of the support of loving relatives. Always it was he who came to them, wherever they could be found.

There was something telling about how in his Washington days, Wilcox remained drawn to the military in his social life and, indeed, in his very manner of speech. Though out of uniform for decades, he carried himself to the end as someone who had been on an arduous and lengthy campaign yet was determined to continue to carry out whatever he was called upon to do, until that command for which the exhausted soldier longs was finally given: "Dismissed."

NOTES

INTRODUCTION

1. Total determined from individual service records contained in G. W. Cullum, "Biographical Register of the Officers and Graduates of the U.S. Military Academy from 1802 to 1867" (Boston, 1891), and Ellsworth Eliot, Jr., "West Point in the Confederacy" (New York, 1941).

2. Darius N. Couch, obituary of Cadmus M. Wilcox, included in *Report of 22nd Annual Reunion of the Association of Graduates of the U.S. Military Academy at West Point, N.Y., June 12, 1891* (Saginaw, MI, 1891), 34. (Cited hereafter as Couch.)

Chapter 1. Conquering A Peace

1. Samuel E. Chamberlain, *My Confession* (New York, 1956), 201.

2. Cadmus M. Wilcox, *History of the Mexican War,* ed. Mary Rachel Wilcox (Washington, D.C., 1892), 117.

3. Ibid., 118.

4. Couch, 28; U.S. Military Academy Monthly Class Reports and Conduct Rolls, 1831–1866.

5. Dabney H. Maury, "General T. J. 'Stonewall' Jackson," *Southern Historical Society Papers* 25 (1897): 311–12.

6. Wilcox, *Mexican War,* 471.

7. A. L. Long, *Memoirs of Robert E. Lee* (New York, 1886), 66.

8. Wilcox, *Mexican War,* 560–61.

9. Ibid., 511.

10. Ibid., 264.

11. James C. Birdsong, *Brief Sketches of North Carolina Troops in the War Between the States* (Raleigh, 1894), 54.

12. G. Moxley Sorrel, *Recollections of a Confederate Staff Officer,* ed. Bell Irvin Wiley (Jackson, TN, 1958), 92–93.

13. Cullum, "Biographical Register," 302.

14. Joseph B. James, "Life at West Point 100 Years Ago," *Mississippi Valley Historical Review* 31 (June 1944): 36.

15. Mary Emily Wilcox to John A. Wilcox, May 27, 1853, Andrew J. Donelson Papers, Manuscript Division, Library of Congress. (Cited hereafter as Donelson Papers.)

16. Dabney H. Maury, *Recollections of a Virginian in the Mexican, Indian and Civil Wars* (New York, 1894), 50.

17. Special Order 161, November 12, 1857, Adjutant General's Office, National Archives.

18. Cadmus Wilcox to Mary Emily Wilcox, November 26, 1861, Cadmus Wilcox Papers, Manuscript Division, Library of Congress. (Cited hereafter as Wilcox Papers.)

19. Couch, 30.

20. Cadmus M. Wilcox, *Rifles and Rifle Practice* (New York, 1859), 238–43.

21. *Dictionary of American Biography,* ed. Allen Johnson, Dumas Malone, and Harris E. Starr (New York, 1928–44), vol. 20, 201.

22. Jon L. Wakelyn, *Biographical Dictionary of the Confederacy* (Westport, CT, 1977), 438–39; Chamberlain, *Confession,* 122–23.

23. Cadmus M. Wilcox to Mary Emily Wilcox, January 6, 1860, Donelson Papers.

24. Ibid., n.d.

25. Samuel T. Cushing, "The Acting Signal Corps," *Military Order of the Loyal Legion of the United States* 15 (1892): 94.

26. Richard S. Ewell to Elizabeth S. Ewell, January 22, 1861, Richard S. Ewell Papers, Manuscript Division, Library of Congress.

27. Ibid.

28. Stephen W. Sears, *George B. McClellan, the Young Napoleon* (New York, 1988), 66.

29. Autobiographical fragment, Wilcox Papers; Cadmus Wilcox to Col. L. Thomas, June 8, 1861, Wilcox Papers.

30. Wakelyn, *Biographical Dictionary of the Confederacy*, 438.

31. James T. McIntosh, ed., *The Papers of Jefferson Davis,* vol. 2 (Baton Rouge, LA, 1974), 203.

32. Alice Graham McCollin, "The Sunshine of the White House," *The Ladies' Home Journal* (January 1894): 7.
33. Pauline Wilcox Burke, *Emily Donelson of Tennessee*, vol. 3 (Richmond, 1941), 199.
34. Ibid., vol. 1, 91.
35. Cullum, "Biographical Register," 207.
36. McCollin, "Sunshine," 7.
37. Mary Emily Wilcox to John Donelson, July 5, 1849, Donelson Papers.
38. Mary Emily Wilcox to John Donelson, August 15, 1848, Donelson Papers.
39. McCollin, "Sunshine," 7.
40. "Born in the White House—Romantic Story of the First Child Born under the President's Roof," *Chicago News* (n.d.), Donelson Papers.
41. Andrew J. Donelson to Mary Emily Wilcox, May 26, 1861, Donelson Papers.
42. Ibid.

Chapter 2. A Strange New Army

1. U.S. War Department. *The War of the Rebellion: Official Records of the Union and Confederate Armies,* vol. 51, part 2, 198–99. (Cited hereafter as O.R. All volumes are in series 1 unless otherwise indicated.)
2. Autobiographical fragment, Wilcox Papers.
3. Hilary A. Herbert, "History of the Eighth Alabama Volunteer Regiment, C. S. A.," ed. Maurice S. Fortin, *Alabama Historical Quarterly* 39 (1977): 38.
4. Ibid.
5. Ibid., 44.
6. John C. C. Sanders to Charles P. Sanders, February 3, 1862, John C. C. Sanders Papers, University of Alabama. (Cited hereafter as Sanders Papers.)
7. Bailey Thomson, "John C. C. Sanders: Lee's Boy Brigadier," *Alabama Review* 32 (April 1979): 88.
8. Herbert, "History of the Eighth Alabama," 43.
9. Ibid.
10. John C. C. Sanders, July 16, 1861, Sanders Papers.
11. J. H. Williams, "Wilcox's Brigade at Gaines' Mill," *Confederate Veteran* 8 (1900): 443.
12. George Clark, "Wilcox's Alabama Brigade at Gettysburg," *Confederate Veteran* 17 (1909): 230.

13. George Clark, *A Glance Backward on Some Events in the Past History of My Life* (Houston, TX, 1914), 14.

14. Ibid., 13.

15. Cadmus Wilcox to Mary Emily Wilcox, August 1, 1861, Wilcox Papers.

16. Cadmus Wilcox to Mary Emily Wilcox, September 8, 1861, Wilcox Papers.

17. Cadmus Wilcox to Mary Emily Wilcox, October 11, 1861, Wilcox Papers.

18. Wilcox Confederate Service Record, May 27, 1862, National Archives.

19. Wilcox Confederate Service Record, October 2, 1861, National Archives.

20. Jefferson Davis, *The Papers of Jefferson Davis,* vol. 7, ed. Lynda Lasswell Crist and Mary Seaton Dix (Baton Rouge, LA, 1974 and 1992), 269.

21. Cadmus Wilcox to Mary Emily Wilcox, November 18, 1861, Wilcox Papers.

22. Henry Heth, *The Memoirs of Henry Heth* (Westport, CT, 1974), 152.

23. Cadmus Wilcox to Mary Emily Wilcox, November 28, 1861, Wilcox Papers.

24. Cadmus Wilcox to Mary Emily Wilcox, November 26, 1861, Wilcox Papers.

25, Ibid.

26. Ibid.

27. John C. C. Sanders, July 28, 1861, Sanders Papers.

28. Clark, *A Glance Backward,* 15–16.

29. W. H. Sanders, August 19, 1861, Sanders Papers.

30. Cadmus Wilcox to Mary Emily Wilcox, October 11, 1861, Wilcox Papers.

31. Florence McCarthy letter, December (5?) 1861, McCarthy Family Papers, Virginia Historical Society.

32. Cadmus Wilcox to John A. Wilcox, April 10, 1862, Wilcox Papers.

33. O.R., vol. 11, part 1, 590.

34. Ibid., 592.

35. Ibid., 593.

36. Ibid., 567.

37. Sorrel, *Recollections,* 26.

38. Clark, *A Glance Backward,* 22.

39. O.R., Vol. 11, part 1, 567.

40. Ibid., 986.

41. Ibid., 988.

42. Ibid.

43. Ibid., 989.

44. James Longstreet, *From Manassas to Appomattox* (Bloomington, IN, 1960), 96.

45. Clark, *A Glance Backward,* 21.

46. Cadmus Wilcox to Mary Emily Wilcox, June 7, 1862, Wilcox Papers.

47. Cadmus Wilcox to Mary Emily Wilcox, June 28, 1962, Wilcox Papers.

48. J. H. Williams, "Wilcox's Brigade at Gaines' Mill," *Confederate Veteran* 8 (1900): 443–44.

49. O.R., vol. 11, part 1, 773.

50. Ibid.

51. Ibid., 773–774.

52. Ibid., 774.

53. Clark, *A Glance Backward,* 24.

54. C. Irvine Walker, *Life of Lt. Gen. Richard Heron Anderson* (Charleston, SC, 1917), 88.

55. O.R., vol. 11, part 1, 758.

56. Ibid., 775–79.

57. O.R., vol. 12, part 2, 597.

58. Janet B. Hewett, Noah Andre Trudeau, and Bryce A. Suderow, eds., *Supplement to the Official Records of the Union and Confederate Armies,* vol. 2, part 1 (Wilmington, NC, 1994), 770.

59. Cadmus Wilcox to Mary Emily Wilcox, June 10, 1864, Wilcox Papers.

60. Cadmus Wilcox to Mary Emily Wilcox, October 7, 1862, Wilcox Papers.

61. O.R., vol. 12, part 2, 599.

Chapter 3. Ambition and Discouragement

1. O.R., vol. 51, 634.

2. Cadmus Wilcox to John A. Wilcox, September 26, 1862, Wilcox Papers.

3. Robert E. Lee to Cadmus Wilcox, November 12, 1862, Wilcox Papers.

4. Wilcox Service Record, December 10, 1862, National Archives.

5. Wilcox Service Record, February 6, 1863, National Archives.

6. John S. S. Sanders, February 10, 1863, Sanders Papers.

7. Robert E. Rodes to Richard S. Ewell, March 22, 1863, Polk-Brown-Ewell Papers, Southern Historical Collection, University of North Carolina.
8. Andrew Donelson to Mary Emily Wilcox, September 28, 1861, Donelson Papers.
9. Andrew Donelson to Maj. Gen. Stephen A. Hurlbut, May 29, 1863, Donelson Papers.
10. John B. Jones, *A Rebel War Clerk's Diary* (Philadelphia, 1866), 345.
11. Cadmus Wilcox to Mary Emily Wilcox, February 15, 1862, Wilcox Papers.
12. Cadmus Wilcox to Mary Emily Wilcox, April 25, 1863, Wilcox Papers.
13. John Piney Oden, "The End of Oden's War: A Confederate Captain's Diary," *Alabama Historical Quarterly* 43 (1981): 77.
14. Herbert, "History of the Eighth Alabama," 90–91.
15. Ibid., 100.
16. John S. S. Sanders, February 10, 1863, Sanders Papers.
17. Herbert, "History of the Eighth Alabama," 100.
18. O.R., vol. 25, 858.
19. Ibid., 859.
20. John S. S. Sanders, n.d., Sanders Papers.
21. Ibid.
22. Daniel M. Holt, M.D., *A Surgeon's Civil War: The Letters and Diary of Daniel M. Holt, M.D.* (Kent, OH, 1994), 96.
23. O.R., vol. 25, 859.
24. O.R., vol. 25, 803.
25. Cadmus Wilcox to Mary Emily Wilcox, May 16, 1863, Wilcox Papers.
26. John Piney Oden, "Captain's Diary," 88.
27. Herbert, "History of the Eighth Alabama," 113.
28. Clark, *A Glance Backward*, 229.
29. Herbert, "History of the Eighth Alabama," 113.
30. J. J. Renfroe, 10th Alabama File, Gettysburg National Military Park.
31. O.R., vol. 27, part 2, 618.
32. Herbert, "History of the Eighth Alabama," 117.
33. O.R., vol. 27, part 2, 618.
34. Douglas Southall Freeman, *R. E. Lee: A Biography*, vol. 3 (New York, 1934–35), 555–56.
35. O.R., vol. 27, part 2, 619.
36. W. H. Sanders, July 16, 1863, Sanders Papers.

37. Clark, *A Glance Backward*, 230.
38. Walter Harrison, *Pickett's Men: A Fragment of War History* (New York, 1870), 95–96.
39. Clifford Dowdey, *Death of a Nation* (New York, 1958), 270.
40. O.R., vol. 27, part 2, 620.
41. LaSalle Corbell Pickett, *Pickett and His Men* (Atlanta, 1899), 302.
42. R. A. Bright, "Pickett's Charge," *Southern Historical Society Papers* 31 (1904): 232.
43. Clark, *A Glance Backward*, 40.
44. O.R., vol. 27, part 2, 620.
45. James Arthur Lyon Fremantle, *Three Months in the Southern States* (New York, 1864), 215.
46. W. H. Sanders, July 16, 1863, Sanders Papers.

Chapter 4. Struggle in the Wilderness

1. Autobiographical fragment, Wilcox Papers.
2. John C. C. Sanders, August 30, 1863, Sanders Papers.
3. Abner Perrin to Gov. M. L. Bonham, July 29, 1863, *Mississippi Valley Historical Review* 24 (March 1938): 520.
4. Douglas Southall Freeman, ed., *Lee's Dispatches to Jefferson Davis, 1862–1865* (New York, 1957), 116.
5. George G. Benedict, "The Element of Romance in Military History," *Military Order of the Loyal Legion of the United States* 57 (1994): 76
6. O.R., vol. 29, 868–69.
7. Cadmus Wilcox to Mary Emily Wilcox, August 22, 1863, Wilcox Papers.
8. Cadmus Wilcox to Mary Emily Wilcox, October 27, 1863, Wilcox Papers.
9. "Proceedings of the First Confederate Congress," *Southern Historical Society Papers* 50 (1953): 382.
10. Ezra J. Warner and W. Buck Yearns, *Biographical Register of the Confederate Congress* (Baton Rouge, LA, 1975), 257–58.
11. Cadmus Wilcox to Mary Emily Wilcox, February 8, 1864, Wilcox Papers.
12. *Chicago News,* n.d., Donelson Papers.
13. Cadmus Wilcox to Rachel Donelson, February 8, 1864.
14. Cadmus Wilcox to Ambrose H. Wright, March 26, 1864, Ambrose H. Wright Papers, Duke University.
15. O.R., vol. 33, 1124.

16. William H. McLaurin, "Eighteenth Regiment," *Histories of the Several Regiments and Battalions from North Carolina in the Great War, 1861–1865,* ed. Walter Clark, vol. 2 (Raleigh, 1901), 47.

17. Heth, *Memoirs,* 184.

18. Cadmus Wilcox to Edward Porter Alexander, March 10, 1869, Edward Porter Alexander Papers, University of North Carolina. (Cited hereafter as Alexander Papers.)

19. *Annals of the War, Written by Leading Participants North and South* (Philadelphia, 1879), 495.

20. Freeman, *R. E. Lee,* vol. 3, 286.

21. Ibid.

22. Benedict, "Element of Romance," 75–76.

23. Cadmus Wilcox to Edward Porter Alexander, March 10, 1869, Alexander Papers.

24. Heth, *Memoirs,* 185.

25. Ibid.

26. Ezra J. Warner, *Generals in Gray* (Baton Rouge, LA, 1959), 235.

27. J. William Jones, *Personal Recollections, Anecdotes and Letters of Gen. R. D. Lee* (New York, 1874), 40.

28. Clement A. Evans, ed., *Confederate Military History,* vol. 3 (Atlanta, 1899), 460.

29. Noah Andre Trudeau, *Bloody Roads South: The Wilderness to Cold Harbor, May–June 1864,* (Boston, 1989), 235.

30. John S. Wise, *The End of an Era* (Boston, 1901), 320.

31. St. Clair A. Mulholland, *The Story of the 116th Regiment, Pennsylvania Volunteers in the War of the Rebellion* (New York, 1996), 275.

32. William J. Pegram to Virginia Johnson Pegram McIntosh, June 28, 1864, Pegram-Johnson-McIntosh Papers, Virginia Historical Society.

33. Cadmus Wilcox to Mary Emily Wilcox, August 15, 1864, Wilcox Papers.

34. Cadmus Wilcox to Mary Emily Wilcox, June 7, 1864, Wilcox Papers.

35. Cadmus Wilcox, Petersburg Campaign Report, Lee Headquarters Papers, Virginia Historical Society.

36. Cadmus Wilcox to Mary Emily Wilcox, October 18, 1864, Wilcox Papers.

37. Cadmus Wilcox to Mary Emily Wilcox, November 21, 1864, Wilcox Papers.

38. O.R., vol. 43, 739.

39. Ibid.

40. Ibid., 753.

41. Mrs. Roger Pryor, *My Day: Reminiscences of a Long Life* (New York, 1909), 210–11.
42. Ibid., 211–12.
43. Cadmus Wilcox to Mary Emily Wilcox, February 22, 1865, Wilcox Papers.
44. Ibid.
45. Cadmus Wilcox, "Defence of Batteries Gregg and Whitworth and the Evacuation of Petersburg," *Southern Historical Society Papers* 4 (1877): 21–22.
46. Nelson D. Lankford, "The Diary of Thomas Conolly, M.P.: Lee's Last Days at Petersburg," *Civil War* 14 (September 1988): 54.
47. Ibid.
48. Ibid., 54–55.
49. O.R., vol. 46, part 2, 1315–16.
50. Lankford, "Conolly Diary," 57.
51. James Lane, "Glimpses of Army Life in 1864," *Southern Historical Society Papers* 18 (1890): 421.
52. Lankford, "Conolly Diary," 57.
53. Wilcox, "Defence," 22.
54. Lankford, "Conolly Diary," 58.
55. Wilcox, "Defence," 25.
56. Ibid.
57. Ibid.
58. A. K. Jones, "The Battle of Fort Gregg," *Southern Historical Society Papers* 31 (1903): 58.
59. Burke Davis, *To Appomattox: Nine April Days, 1865* (New York, 1959), 75.
60. Ibid., 76.
61. Wilcox, "Defence," 29.
62. Ibid., 32.
63. Cadmus Wilcox, Petersburg Campaign Report, Lee Headquarters Papers.
64. Joshua L. Chamberlain, "Appomattox, a Paper Read by . . . , October 7, 1903," *Military Order of the Loyal Legion of the United States* 22 (1907): 270.
65. John Gibbon, *Personal Recollections of the Civil War* (New York, 1928), 318.
66. Ibid., 320.
67. Wesley Merritt, "The Appomattox Campaign," *Military Order of the Loyal Legion of the United States* 14 (1892): 128–29.
68. Autobiographical fragment, Wilcox Papers.

69. Chamberlain, "Appomattox," 270.
70. Long, *Memoirs of Robert E. Lee,* 426–27.

Chapter 5. "He Did His Whole Duty"
1. Edward Porter Alexander, *Military Memoirs of a Confederate* (New York, 1907), 614.
2. Ibid., 614–15.
3. Ibid., 615.
4. Wilcox, "Defence," 22.
5. Joseph Howard Parks, *General Edmund Kirby Smith, C.S.A.* (Baton Rouge, LA, 1992), 481–82.
6. Andrew Wilcox to Andrew J. Donelson, July 23, 1865, Donelson Papers.
7. Parks, *General Edmund Kirby Smith,* 481.
8. Andrew F. Rolls, *The Lost Cause: The Confederate Exodus to Mexico* (Norman, OK, 1965), 54.
9. Robert E. Lee to Cadmus M. Wilcox, December 23, 1865, Lee Headquarters Papers.
10. Camille Baquet, *History of the First Brigade, New Jersey Volunteers from 1861 to 1865* (Trenton, 1910), 251.
11. Couch, 33.
12. Richard S. Ewell to Mrs. Ewell, February 14, 1870, Brown-Ewell Papers, Tennessee State Library and Archives.
13. Daniel Harvey Hill, Editorial, *Land We Love* 1 (November 1868): 87.
14. Cadmus Wilcox to Edward Porter Alexander, March 10, 1869, Alexander Papers.
15. Ibid.; *Southern Historical Society Papers* 6 (1878): 244.
16. Cadmus Wilcox to Edward Porter Alexander, March 10, 1869, Alexander Papers.
17. Ibid., February 6, 1869.
18. *Chicago News,* n.d., Donelson Papers.
19. Couch, 33.
20. *Official Register of the United States* (1879); *New York Times,* December 3, 1890.
21. *Official Register of the United States* (1881).
22. Harrison Adreon to Cadmus M. Wilcox, April 22, 1879, Wilcox Papers.
23. Cadmus Wilcox to Jane Claudia Saunders Johnson, June 6, 1889, B. T. Johnson Manuscripts, Duke University.

24. Couch, 33.
25. Unidentified newspaper clipping bylined "Vanity Fair," (n.d.), Donelson Papers.
26. Cadmus Wilcox, "Gen. C. M. Wilcox on the Battle of Gettysburg," *Southern Historical Society Papers* 5 (1878): 146–47.
27. Cadmus Wilcox to D. H. Hill, June 23, 1885, D. H. Hill Papers, Virginia State Library.
28. Longstreet, *Manassas to Appomattox,* 108–9.
29. *Philadelphia Weekly Times,* November 24, 1877.
30. Glenn Tucker, *Hancock the Superb* (Indianapolis, 1960), 304; Sears, *McClellan, the Young Napoleon,* 397; Aztec Club File, Manuscript Division, U.S. Army Military History Institute, Carlisle, Pennsylvania.
31. Cadmus Wilcox to Virginia Caroline (Tunstall) Clay, July 18, 1886, Virginia Caroline (Tunstall) Clay Manuscripts, Duke University.
32. Cadmus Wilcox to John W. Daniel, January 25, 1876, Daniel Papers, Duke University.
33. Aztec Club File.
34. Mary Emily Wilcox to Grover Cleveland, May 21, 1885, Donelson Papers.
35. McCollin, "Sunshine," 7.
36. Cadmus Wilcox to Virginia Caroline (Tunstall) Clay, July 5, 1886, Clay Manuscripts.
37. Cadmus Wilcox to Virginia Caroline (Tunstall) Clay, June 24, 1890, Clay Manuscripts.
38. *Washington Post,* December 3, 1890.
39. Ibid.
40. Publisher's promotional literature, Wilcox Papers.
41. *New York Times,* December 3, 1890.
42. Couch, 34–35.
43. Cadmus Wilcox to Mary Emily Wilcox, April 24, 1863, Wilcox Papers.

BIBLIOGRAPHY

Manuscript Sources
University of Alabama, Tuscaloosa, Alabama
    John S. S. Sanders Papers
    W. H. Sanders Papers

Duke University, Durham, North Carolina
    Benson-Thompson Family Papers
    Virginia Caroline (Tunstall) Clay Manuscripts
    John W. Daniel Papers
    B. T. Johnson Papers
    Charles C. Jones, Jr., Papers
    Ambrose H. Wright Papers

Library of Congress, Washington, DC
    Andrew J. Donelson Papers
    Richard S. Ewell Papers
    Cadmus Wilcox Papers

National Archives, Washington, DC
    Wilcox Service Record

University of North Carolina, Chapel Hill, North Carolina
    Edward Porter Alexander Papers
    Polk-Brown-Ewell Papers

Tennessee State Library and Archives, Nashville
  Brown-Ewell Papers

Virginia Historical Society, Richmond
  Lee Headquarters Papers
  McCarthy Family Papers
  Pegram-Johnson-McIntosh Papers

Virginia State Library, Richmond
  D. H. Hill Papers

University of Virginia, Charlottesville, Virginia
  The Rev. J. William Jones Papers

NEWSPAPERS
Chicago News, n.d.
New York Times, 1890.
Philadelphia Weekly Times, 1877.
Southern Illustrated News, Richmond, 1864.
Washington Post, 1890.

OFFICIAL PUBLICATIONS
Biographical Directory of the American Congress, 1774–1971. Washington,
  DC, 1971.
U.S. State Department. *Official Register of the United States.* Washington, DC.
U.S. War Department. *War of the Rebellion: Official Records of the Union
  and Confederate Armies.* 128 vols. Washington, DC, 1880–1901.

BOOKS
Alexander, Edward Porter. *Military Memoirs of a Confederate.* New York,
  1907.
Baquet, Camille. *History of the First Brigade, New Jersey Volunteers from
  1861 to 1865.* Trenton, 1910.
Bridsong, James C. *Brief Sketches of North Carolina Troops in the War
  Between the States.* Raleigh, NC, 1894.
Burke, Pauline Wilcox. *Emily Donelson of Tennessee.* Richmond, 1941.

Chamberlain, Samuel E. *My Confession*. New York, 1956.

Clark, George. *A Glance Backward on Some Events in the Past History of My Life*. Houston, TX, 1914.

Clark, Walter. *Histories of the Several Regiments and Battalions from North Carolina in the Great War, 1861–1865*. 5 vols. Raleigh, NC, 1901.

Clayton, W. W. *History of Davidson County, Tenn.* Philadelphia, 1880.

Cullum, G. W. *Biographical Register of the Officers and Graduates of the U.S. Military Academy from 1802 to 1867*. Boston, 1891.

Davis, Burke. *To Appomattox: Nine April Days, 1865*. New York, 1959.

Davis, Jefferson. *The Papers of . . .* Vol. 2 of 9, edited by James T. McIntosh, and vol. 7, edited by Lynda Lasswell Crist and Mary Seaton Dix. Baton Rouge, LA, 1974 and 1992.

Dowdey, Clifford. *Death of a Nation*. New York, 1958.

Eliot, Ellsworth, Jr., *West Point in the Confederacy*. New York, 1941.

Evans, Clement A., ed. *Confederate Military History*. 13 vols. Atlanta, 1889.

Fremantle, James Arthur Lyon. *Three Months in the Southern States*. New York, 1864.

Freeman, Douglas Southall, ed. *Lee's Dispatches to Jefferson Davis, 1861–1865*. New York, 1957.

———. *Lee's Lieutenants*. 3 vols. New York, 1945.

———. *R. E. Lee: A Biography*. 4 vols. New York, 1934–35.

Gibbon, John. *Personal Recollections of the Civil War*. New York, 1928.

Harrison, Walter. *Pickett's Men: A Fragment of War History*. New York, 1870.

Heth, Henry. *The Memoirs of Henry Heth*. Westport, CT, 1974.

Hewett, Janet B., Noah Andre Trudeau, and Bryce A. Suderow, eds. *Supplement to the Official Records of the Union and Confederate Armies*. Wilmington, NC, 1994.

Jones, John B. *A Rebel War Clerk's Diary*. Philadelphia, 1866.

Kerby, Robert L. *Kirby Smith's Confederacy: The Trans-Mississippi South, 1863–1865*. Tuscaloosa, AL, 1972.

Long, A. L. *Memoirs of Robert E. Lee*. New York, 1886.

Longstreet, James. *From Manassas to Appomattox*. Bloomington, IN, 1960.

Maury, Dabney H. *Recollections of a Virginian in the Mexican, Indian and Civil War*. New York, 1894.

Mulholland, St. Clair A. *The Story of the 116th Regiment, Pennsylvania Volunteers in the War of the Rebellion*. New York, 1996.

Parks, Joseph Howard. *General Edmund Kirby Smith, C.S.A.* Baton Rouge, LA, 1992.

Pfanz, Donald C. *Richard S. Ewell: A Soldier's Life.* Chapel Hill, NC, 1998.
Pickett, LaSalle Corbell. *Pickett and His Men.* Atlanta, 1899.
Pryor, Mrs. Roger A. *My Day: Reminiscences of a Long Life.* New York, 1909.
Rolls, Andrew F. *The Lost Cause: The Confederate Exodus to Mexico.* Norman, OK, 1965.
Sears, Stephen W. *George B. McClellan, the Young Napoleon.* New York, 1988.
Sorrel, G. Moxley. *Recollections of a Confederate Staff Officer.* Edited by Bell Irvin Wiley. Jackson, TN, 1958
Trudeau, Noah Andre. *Bloody Roads South: The Wilderness to Cold Harbor, May–June 1864.* Boston, 1989.
Tucker, Glenn. *Hancock the Superb.* Indianapolis, 1960.
Wakelyn, Jon L. *Biographical Dictionary of the Confederacy.* Westport, CT, 1977.
Walker, C. Irvine. *Life of Lt. Gen. Richard Heron Anderson.* Charleston, SC, 1917.
Warner, Ezra J. *Generals in Gray.* Baton Rouge, LA, 1959.
Warner, Ezra J., and W. Buck Yearns. *Biographical Register of the Confederate Congress.* Baton Rouge, LA, 1975.
Wilcox, Cadmus M. *History of the Mexican War.* Edited by Mary Rachel Wilcox. Washington, DC, 1892.
———. *Rifles and Rifle Practice.* New York, 1859.
Wise, John A. *The End of an Era.* Boston, 1901.

Articles

Benedict, George G. "The Element of Romance in Military History." *Military Order of the Loyal Legion of the United States* 57 (1994): 59–77.
Bright, R. A. "Pickett's Charge." *Southern Historical Society Papers* 31 (1904): 228–36.
Chamberlain, Joshua L. "Appomattox, a Paper Read by Joshua L. Chamberlain. *Military Order of the Loyal Legion of the United States* (1907): 260–280.
Clark, George. "Wilcox's Alabama Brigade at Gettysburg." *Confederate Veteran* 17 (1909): 229–30.
Couch, Darius N. Obituary of Cadmus M. Wilcox, included in *Report of 22nd Annual Reunion of the Association of Graduates of the U.S. Military Academy at West Point, N.Y., June 12, 1891,* 27–36.

Herbert, Hilary A. "History of the Eighth Alabama Volunteer Regiment, C.S.A." Edited by Maurice S. Fortin. *Alabama Historical Quarterly* 39 (1977): 5–125.

Hill, Daniel Harvey. Editorial. *Land We Love.* 1 (November 1868): 87.

James, Joseph B. "Life at West Point 100 Years Ago." *Mississippi Valley Historical Review* 31 (June 1944).

Jones, A. K. "The Battle of Fort Gregg." *Southern Historical Society Papers* 31 (1903): 56–60.

Lane, James. "Glimpses of Army Life in 1864." *Southern Historical Society Papers* 18 (1890): 406–22.

Lankford, Nelson D. "The Diary of Thomas Conolly, M.P.: Lee's Last Days at Petersburg." *Civil War* 14 (Sept. 1988): 53–63.

Maury, Dabney H. "General T. J. 'Stonewall' Jackson." *Southern Historical Society Papers* 25 (1897): 309–14.

McCollin, Alice Graham. "The Sunshine of the White House." *Ladies Home Journal* (January 1894): 7.

Merritt, Wesley. "The Appomattox Campaign." *Military Order of the Loyal Legion of the United States* 14 (1892): 108–31.

Oden, John Piney. "The End of Oden's War: A Confederate Captain's Diary." Edited by Michael Barton. *Alabama Historical Quarterly* 43 (1981): 73–98.

Thomson, Bailey. "John C. C. Sanders: Lee's 'Boy Brigadier.'" *Alabama Review* 32 (April 1979): 83–107.

Wilcox, Cadmus M. "Defence of Batteries Gregg and Whitworth and the Evacuation of Petersburg." *Southern Historical Society Papers* 4 (1875): 19–33.

———. "Gen. C. M. Wilcox on the Battle of Gettysburg." *Southern Historical Society Papers* 5 (1878): 97–124.

Williams, J. H. "Wilcox's Brigade at Gaines' Mill." *Confederate Veteran* 8 (1900): 443–44.

INDEX